Man Bites
Log

Man Bites Log

The Unlikely Adventures of a City Guy in the Woods

Max Alexander

CARROLL & GRAF PUBLISHERS
NEW YORK

MAN BITES LOG

Carroll & Graf Publishers
An Imprint of Avalon Publishing Group Inc.
245 West 17th Street
New York, NY 10011

AVALON
publishing group incorporated

First Carroll & Graf edition 2004

Library of Congress Cataloging-in-Publication Data is available.

ISBN: 0-7867-1412-3

Printed in the United States of America
Interior design by Maria Elias
Distributed by Publishers Group West

For Sarah, the heartwood

Man Bites Log

Foreword

(Some Notes on Antecedents)

Short of being lost at sea or swept off the north face of Everest, no human calamity has inspired as much modern literature as the purchase of a New England farm. As soon as barns sag, stone walls collapse, and cellars flood, over the horizon comes a writer from New York seeking the simple life, book contract and pitchfork in hand. Like so many New England writers before me, I'm learning that living simply is a complicated business—and living in rural Maine is both inspiring and daunting. Every day I thank God that I'm here, just before I wonder why the hell I'm here, miles from anyone I once knew. At least I have plenty of company on my night table, piled high with back-to-the-land literature.

Weeding and writing, fence repair and poetry would not seem kindred pursuits, yet so many writers have taken up the hammer and hoe that their idylls constitute a literary sub-genre. The back-to-nature theme in American letters dates back to Thoreau, of course, but the modern incarnation took hold in the 1940s—a reaction perhaps to urbanization and the demise of family farming—and the best of those books have gotten a second wind.

The war years in Down East Maine were chronicled brilliantly by transplanted New Yorker E. B. White in his classic

1944 collection *One Man's Meat*, reissued in 1997. And in 1942, a former Boston schoolteacher named Louise Dickinson Rich published *We Took to the Woods*, an account of her life in the Maine backcountry that became an improbable bestseller and prompted two sequels, all of which are in print. Also available in recent paperback reissues are two seminal works from 1948: Henry Beston's *Northern Farm* (also set in Maine) and Elliot Merrick's *Green Mountain Farm*. Merrick was a Manhattan novelist (his editor was the great Maxwell Perkins) who bought his Vermont place for $1,000 during the Depression. "We did everything wrong, but it came out right," he wrote.

But like the stout laconic farmhand named Zeke who always pops up in these books when a cow needs worming, Merrick was savvier than he let on. Possessed of no agricultural knowledge yet determined to farm, he wisely invested in a house unheatable, a barn uninhabitable even by the standards of livestock, land unarable, and (at no extra charge) neighbors incorrigible. In short, he had the perfect setting for a literary reflection on the travails of rural life. His and other tales of woe, including S. J. Perelman's hilarious *Acres and Pains* (first published in 1943 and reissued in 1999), comfort this recent back-to-the-lander, who likewise worries nightly that it was all a terrible mistake.

Mind you, I don't regret leaving nice homes and big offices in New York and Los Angeles for a hundred-and-fifty-year-old farmhouse in backcountry Maine. Today I work at home writing (when I'm not cleaning out the henhouse in rubber boots), for which I earn less money, and cook dinner for my family every night.

No, my constant regrets about our rural adventure center on the nagging suspicion that, like Merrick, we too did everything wrong. Our property, a parcel of inexact acreage slightly larger than the Vatican City and slightly smaller than the Forbidden City, is mostly woods. It looked great from the road when we first pulled up with the real estate agent, but a closer inspection (after the closing) revealed that except for a sly buffer ringing the blueberry field, most of our forest had been denuded by logging over the last few decades. The kindling-sized growth of aspens that remained, quaking in terror, would likely have been ground into pulp as well, had we not come along. My vision of sleigh rides under a canopy of stately sugar maples was dashed as I tromped through the snow, hugging trees with my forefinger.

Leaner still was the local economic landscape. While much of Maine was thriving when we moved here in 1999, the first indication that our corner of the Pine Tree State was not on the Economic Miracle World Tour came when my wife Sarah and I set out to secure home delivery of a newspaper. After years reading the *Times* in a backward-facing car of the Metro North train, I looked forward to leafing through the page-one jumps in my armchair. Hell, we could even get the *Globe* . . .

We could—if we lived anywhere else in Maine. As it happens, not a single one of our hundred fifty acres is on the route of either the *Times* or the *Globe*. We can't even get the Portland paper. At any rate folks in our little town don't much bother about what happens on Murray Hill or Beacon Hill, and I find myself caring less every day; the sheep shed needs a roof and the orchard needs pruning.

There's always the Internet, which is how I now read the *Times* as well as make a living. That would come as no surprise to Merrick, who died in 1997 at age 92. "In this age of electric motors, rapid travel, and communication," he wrote in 1948, "there are more opportunities in the country than there are in the city for enterprising men and women whose principal capital is independence and energy."

He was wrong, of course: what's left of rural America grew poorer over the last half century. But Merrick's enthusiasm for the dicey entrepreneurship known as farming reflects a central theme in back-to-the-land literature: a belief that doing it yourself is better than having it done for you, no matter the result.

Perhaps that explains the millennial popularity of these adventures. At a time when every aspect of life is advised and controlled by experts and their computers (who in turn require their own experts and computers), these books say, in effect, it's okay to grow your own. What follows is my attempt to update the genre for a new era of angst. If I can make something grow in this fertile field—I have no farm-hand named Zeke—at least I won't have done everything wrong.

Introduction

Max, this is Warren Beatty."

I recognized the voice on the phone from countless dark cinemas, and made a mental note to store the conversation in the part of my brain reserved for name dropping at dinner parties.

"Hi, Warren." We had never met or spoken before, but years working as an entertainment journalist in New York and Los Angeles had taught me the protocol. In Hollywood, where phony familiarity is so normal as to be genuine, everyone is first-name.

"Loved the movie, Warren."

For once this was the truth. It was 1998; Beatty's new film, *Bulworth*, was a flawed but stinging satire of contemporary American politics that took a broad swipe at media cynicism for good measure. In the film, Senator Bulworth attacks mass media companies that create all the magazines and newspapers and movies and TV shows and books and music. Beatty wasn't just biting the hand that fed him—he was gnawing on it. The Hollywood grapevine said 20th-Century Fox, a division of Rupert Murdoch's giant News Corp, wasn't exactly pulling out the stops to market the film. So Beatty was stumping hard to get free publicity, which is why he called me. As the editor at *People* magazine in charge of movie coverage, I was the gatekeeper for cover stories on big stars. Decisions made by myself and my boss determined whose face would stare out from the checkout racks at every grocery shopper in America.

"You *really* liked it?" Beatty asked, knowing that praise for a film is one of the more common Hollywood lies. "Well, what do I have to do for the cover?"

He was getting right to the point, which was the hard part. Expecting his call, I already had marching orders from my boss Carol Wallace, the managing editor of the magazine—and Beatty wasn't going to like them. Wallace, who had come up from tabloid dailies, rarely went to movies and had no interest in movie studio machinations. Her reaction was knee-jerk: "Our readers don't like him," she snapped. (Magazine editors always ascribe their personal opinions to readers they've never met.) "They think he's a womanizer. But they'd be interested to see him as a family man. Tell him we need a hometake with Annette and the kids, or no deal."

I gulped. Shooting stars at home—wackily tossing pasta or rough-housing on the couch—was a *People* trademark but an increasingly tough sell; high-profile stalking cases made celebrities more guarded about their private space. And photographing their children was the request from hell. "Can we protect the kids?" I asked Wallace.

"Tell Beatty we can shoot the kids from behind, no faces. But we need to see him doing something with them—reading or playing ball or . . . what*ever* he does," she blurted, waving her arm dismissively. "You're a dad, figure it out."

"Here's the deal," I told Beatty, forcing the words as I

gazed out my three picture windows, thirty-one floors above Sixth Avenue. In the rigid hierarchy of the Time Life Building, I was sitting pretty. Mere writers had to settle for one or maybe two windows. I had a good office, extensive benefits, and an annual bonus, and I could casually mention to my wife after dinner: "Talked to Warren Beatty today."

Of course, that would presume I arrived home before Sarah was already sound asleep—a rare occurrence for an editor at *People*. I swiveled my chair and gave Beatty a list of the magazine's conditions. When I got to the part about the kids, I heard a weary sigh through the receiver, but I plowed ahead: "If you're concerned about security for your children," I added quickly, "don't worry. We won't show their faces."

"Max," Beatty replied calmly after another long sigh. "I'm not worried about kidnappers. I can assure you my family has plenty of security. The issue is much more basic. I simply won't make my children part of the marketing campaign of a movie—any movie. I don't take them to premieres; I don't even let them watch me on the Oscars." He paused to allow the full weight of that statement to sink in. "This may seem hard to believe, but I really don't want my kids to grow up thinking movies are important. I want them to have a childhood that has nothing to do with this business."

"I understand, Warren."

Again it was the truth. I thought about my own two kids, and the efforts of myself and Sarah (a former actress turned schoolteacher) to give them a life of genuine experience over the virtual kids' world created by the experts in Hollywood.

I didn't always feel that way. When I first started covering showbiz as a freelance writer for the *New York Times* in 1987, I thought it was the assignment to die for. Most of my journalism friends were covering town council meetings, or writing about personal finance; I got to interview Martin Scorsese and go to Manhattan premieres. Soon I was hired at *Variety*, the showbiz trade paper, where I rose to executive editor. I bought a tuxedo. I voted for the Tony Awards, and lunched at the Russian Tea Room. Sometimes I even yelled at waiters, and not just in France. I was apprenticing to be an asshole.

To further my studies, there was only one place to go.

When *Variety* moved to Hollywood in 1994, I moved my family too, buying a house in the soon-to-be trendy Los Feliz district of Hollywood. Liz Smith lamented our move in her column, saying how much New Yorkers would miss "the Alexander family." (I had met her once, at a party where I saw Mike Wallace goose Beverly Sills, and when Liz realized I wasn't someone important she walked away. She never met my family.)

In California, showbiz came to define not just my professional life but our family life as well. Our four-year-old boy had an agent *and* a manager, who took him around to auditions for primetime TV shows. (His full-page fashion ads in the *New York Times* were larger than any story I'd ever written for that paper.) All our friends and neighbors were in some way involved in creating mass entertainment—producers, sound men, actors, agents, writers. Sarah and I went to the Emmys, the Grammys, the Oscars. I flew to our offices in London and Paris twice a year, curled up in seat 1-A, dining on foie gras and $100 bottles of Nuits St. Georges. The trips blend together in my brain, but surreal moments stand out: escorting Kate Winslet around the Piazza San Marco during the Venice Film Festival; sitting next to Jack Nicholson during lunch at the island palazzo of an Italian count, while the star loudly pretended our host was performing fellatio on him; scooping up ladlefuls of triple-0 beluga caviar from a mound the size of a Thanksgiving turkey, on a Mediterranean yacht owned by a Russian film tycoon.

Back home I cut the grass, took out the trash, left for work before my kids woke up and drove in traffic jams down Sunset Boulevard. By the time I dragged myself home from the office, everyone was asleep as usual. It was a Cinderella life familiar to any showbiz journalist, and the frayed excess was starting to bother me. Meanwhile, Sarah was becoming attracted to Waldorf education, a private-school movement founded in Germany after World War I by the philosopher Rudolf Steiner. Like many new parents, Sarah and I had started to wonder if the public schools were teaching our kids how to think for themselves, or just teaching them how to pass tests. We weren't alone; by the time Waldorf caught up with us, it had become the largest non-parochial private-school movement in the world. Among Steiner's many perceptions was that children in the industrial age were being denied an education rooted in natural observation. It was deeply spiritual without being dogmatic, and its rejection of unfettered materialism in favor of a more thoughtful path seemed ahead of its time.

Sarah longed to teach at a Waldorf school, but where?

There were plenty of Waldorf schools in Southern California, but we were already thinking of Maine, where Sarah's parents live and where we had been married in 1986. We loved the state's rugged coast, rolling farms, and relative isolation from the mainstream. One night we went to see Garrison Keillor at the Hollywood Bowl, and in the midst of one of his Lake Wobegon reveries he gently reminded us: "Warm weather makes people dumb." That was the moment. Within a month we had a plan to return to New York, where Sarah could get her Master's degree at a small Waldorf teaching school. From there we could more easily strike out for Maine, in search of a new life.

Meanwhile, I was flunking my studies as a Hollywood jerk, despite having some masterful professors. Stranded at Venice's Marco Polo airport as Alitalia pilots went on strike one year, I heard a Hollywood executive screaming at an Italian ticket clerk: "Do you know who I *am*? I'm *Mel Gibson's agent!*" (The pilots stayed on strike.) During a black-tie AIDS benefit in the South of France at the famed Moulin des Mougins, I watched Elizabeth Taylor casually feed the restaurant's three-star Michelin morsels to her lapdog.

Soon we were back in New York and I was working at *People*, where stars and their dogs weren't so much celebrated as fetishized. Even celebrity pets had to reveal their age, which was then earnestly fact-checked with a publicist.

Warren Beatty promised to call back but didn't. The cover story never happened. *Bulworth* flopped. Only our closest friends knew it, but the Alexander family was already planning to exit, stage north.

Author's Note

The chapters in this book—journal entries, in a
sense—were written approximately once a month
over the course of five years beginning in 1999.
Most appeared, in different form, in the *Portland Phoenix*, an
offshoot of the venerable Boston alternative weekly. I have
revised and updated all the stories, but in general retained the
present tense of the original writings.

Evil does not grow in the soil,
nor does trouble grow out of the ground.
No! Man brings trouble on himself,
as surely as sparks fly up from a fire.
                                    The Book of Job

A fool and his farm are soon united.
                                    Anonymous

A Real
Shit Sandwich

(The First Year)

1

Most of my neighbors have never moved in their lives. They certainly never moved to Maine; many have no knowledge of ancestors coming from anyplace else. They speak slowly but are hard to understand, and drive slower but are impossible to pass. Their last name is the same as the road they live on, or the nearby pond. They know everyone who has owned your house since the Civil War. They are almost without exception poor, but they are not looking for sympathy. For these old-time Mainers, the state slogan is irrelevant. "The way life should be" is simply the way life is.

Here is how it is for my neighbor Janet, who first showed up at my door one weekday last August when I was home alone writing. Janet, a stout, truncated woman of around sixty, had walked from her place up the road and was clearly winded from the quarter-mile trek. "My legs ain't so good after my bypass," she said between gasping breaths. I later learned Janet also suffered from diabetes, a common ailment here where preventive health care is virtually unknown. She glanced around the house at the sawdust piles. "You're doin' a lot of work here, eh?"

"Place really needed it," I said, somehow defensively.

" 'Twas for sale a long time," she offered, stretching out the word "long" into several measures and implying that in these parts, it takes a while for the right sucker to come along.

"I guess they saw us coming," I said distractedly. I had a lot of work to do, and I was in no mood for a second opinion on our new home, which I was trying valiantly to pretend I liked. The day before, our plumber—another native Mainer and a diabetic who appeared to get ornery when his blood sugar dropped—called our house "a real shit sandwich" and suggested we consider burning it for the insurance. He ripped out a few perfectly good fixtures before peeling off in a cloud of gravel dust for the local stock car races. No, it wasn't a good day for Janet. But neighbors, like relatives, are entitled to relaxed visiting hours, so I found her a chair and was glad when she immediately changed the subject to her life story.

The walking tour of Janet's days could have been described in metes and bounds from my doorstep. She grew up in Waldoboro, a village down the road; moving up here decades ago with her husband, Cliff, constituted a major emigration. "I started work at the light bulb factory when I was eighteen, and I retired forty years later," Janet said without a trace of pride or remorse. (For decades the Sylvania company employed locals at its light bulb plant in Waldoboro.) "My son almost died when he was sixteen." It was the first of many non-sequiturs that I came to understand as her conversational tick.

"How awful. What happened?"

"He was working under a truck that was up on blocks. Another guy was under the hood with a screwdriver and touched the starter wire. That truck jumped right off them blocks and landed on my boy."

"Oh my Lord. What a miracle that he survived."

"The doctor said it was because he had just eaten lunch. You want some corn?"

"Corn?"

"My husband, he's got a big garden. Lots of corn. Come over and get some if you want. Much as you want. He had a bypass too. Now he's got colon cancer."

My family had arrived too late in the season to start our own garden, so a few days later I found myself standing with Cliff—a slight yet rugged old man with small eyes and a deeply burnished tan—in a cornrow humming with mosquitoes. We filled a few paper bags and moved on to the beet greens. Cliff and I chatted about the drought as he carefully scraped the roots and dirt off each marble-sized beet with a pocket knife before dropping it in a bag for me. "I've got colon cancer," he finally said. "Going down to Portland tomorrow for some tests."

I expressed sympathy but he just shrugged, and stooped to pull another beet. "Whatever happens, happens. It's not like a young person; I've lived a good life. No sense worrying about it."

After forcing him to stop filling bags, I left with eleven cucumbers, three cauliflowers, one cabbage, ten pounds of potatoes (weighed later at home), two pounds of beet greens, nineteen ear of corn and a gallon jar of homemade pickles.

The next day, I baked a gratin out of their cauliflower and brought it over to Cliff and Janet. I had not yet learned that in rural Maine, the giving of homegrown vegetables is meant to relieve the grower of foodstuffs, thus lessening the number of meals that must be prepared—and meals must definitely be prepared from whatever has grown, since food on the farm can never be wasted. Returning the gift, even transformed in a cooked dish, is counter-productive. To give, in this case, is not to receive. But Janet took it graciously. "We'll get this dish back right quick," she said as I handed over the still-warm dinner.

"No sense worrying about it," I said.

When Janet returned the dish a few days later, it contained a homemade mincemeat pie. Checkmate. Game point. Serve returned. I surrendered, and admired the pie. Although a genuine meat dish in Colonial times, mincemeat pies have been made with raisins and nuts since the nineteenth century. Not Janet's. She still made hers with meat. The meat was venison. She shot the deer. "If I get lucky this winter," she called out as she headed up the road, "I'll make you one with moose."

Later that year, Cliff had his cancerous colon removed. Janet died on Valentine's Day of 2002, at age sixty-two. In the spring of 2004, Cliff was out again, planting beet greens.

2

Contrary to popular belief, money grows on trees in Maine; just ask any logger. You could look one up, or you could buy one hundred fifty acres of forest and wait a week.

The first woodsman pulled up early last July, a few days after our moving truck departed. A hulking, boisterous fellow in his twenties, he bounded up the steps to our kitchen door, biceps popping out of his t-shirt. "Evening, sir!" he shouted through the twilight, apparently unused to conversation without a chainsaw running. "Somebody finally bought this old place, eh? Name's Willard Pierpont. Just came by to welcome you to the neighborhood."

He wasn't dropping off pound cake, but I invited him in and wondered how soon he would get to the point. "By the way," he said, stepping over the threshold, "I just happen to be in the timber business with my father. He knows all a-these woods, and he says that your land hasn't been cut in over seventy years."

"Actually, it was cut in nineteen eighty-one," I said. "They left the blackberry brambles."

"Oh, I don't mean *this* side of the road," he said, guffawing at my idiocy as he gestured out the window. "Nothing out there but pulp, and that market's in the toilet. I mean your land over there," pointing across the road.

"Well, I only have fifteen acres over there."

"Oh, I know what you got," he said, chuckling again at my inability to recognize his all-seeing knowledge of my land. "Been walking through there myself—uh, hope you don't mind, it ain't posted or nothin'. Big white pines, three foot wide, maybe two hundred years old, You stand to make thousands off that lot."

"I was thinking of leaving it alone," I said, feeling inexplicably stupid. "Sort of a wildlife refuge."

"Bad idea!" said Willard. "Deer actually prefer a cut woods; gives 'em new tree sprouts to browse on. Of course, we'd do a *selective* cut—mainly clear out them big pines hit by lightnin'."

I was no expert, but I suspected trees riven into splinters by lightning had limited value as saw timber. I told him I'd been thinking of hiring a forester to plot a strategy, and he scoffed. "A good logger will do the same thing, no charge," he said. I told him I'd consider his offer as he stepped into the night, swatting fireflies.

Which explains how I found myself one February morning tramping through my woods on snowshoes with two dogs, a compass, and a woman named Barrie Brusila, licensed Maine forester. As it happened, it was a good time to hire her. The state hadn't spent all the money it allocated for cleanup from the 1998 ice storm, so it was doling out the cash to woodlot owners like myself who agreed to set up a ten-year forest management plan.

"I bet he said foresters are a waste of money, huh?" Barrie asked when I mentioned Willard. Part of her job is working with loggers, and she understands their business, even if her background is very different from the backwoods types who have cut trees around here for generations. After growing up in Massachusetts and Maryland, she caused a minor family scandal by dropping out of Wellesley to pursue forestry at the University of Maine. Her family is proud of her work now, she says—and she doesn't regret her undergrad years as a psychology major. "It comes in handy when dealing with loggers," she notes.

Unlike forestry—an appealing mix of academics and outdoor life—logging is not exactly a crowded table at the job fair. Woodsmen work hard for low profit margins, using incredibly deadly tools. The U.S. Department of Labor recently cited logging as the most dangerous job in America—beating out commercial fishing and police work. And like beleaguered farmers, the value of a logger's "crop" is dictated by middlemen and market forces way beyond his control. It's not uncommon for a logger to work sixty-hour weeks just to get by. On the other hand, today's logger brings technology into the woods that is capable of devastation undreamed of by the axe-toting woodsman of yore. The temptation to exceed can be great.

Foresters also bring powerful technology to the woods. The hundreds of tree measurements we made during two days in my forest will be fed into Barrie's computer, which will create a detailed profile of my timber inventory. That information will be useful to plan conservation efforts—or responsible logging. Indeed, owning this much land has given me a sense of responsibility and purpose that I haven't felt since my kids were born.

The state hopes a management plan will avoid a repeat of what happened on my property in 1981. "Your land was logged in a technique called high-grading," said Barrie as we trudged forward on our snowshoes, measuring trees along pre-plotted cruise lines. "Basically, that means they cut all the good wood and left the crap. It's fairly typical on small wood-lots, where the homeowner isn't out there watching the job."

The only bright spot was that whoever cut my land was lazy; he avoided difficult-to-reach areas like high ground and the abundant wetlands, all of which are still thick with older, wildlife-sustaining trees including hardwoods like oak and ash.

It was along part of my wetland that we discovered one of the largest beaver habitats Barrie had ever seen, including a dam more than fifty feet long. Nature's loggers had left a starkly beautiful wasteland of chewed-off tree stumps. But the lack of freshly nibbled trees told Barrie that the beavers were gone—trapped out for their valuable pelts. (Not just loggers see dollar signs in the Maine woods.) "They'll come back," she said, "because the habitat is ideal. But you need to post your land, or the trappers will be back too."

Posting land is a sensitive issue here, as I was about to learn. Native Mainers almost never put up "No Trespassing" signs, which are considered an insult to neighbors and sportsmen. According to the state's hunting regulations, unposted land is deemed open for hunting and trapping, which is the way most people like it around here. Unfortu-nately, the proliferation of all-terrain vehicles has compli-cated the issue; I didn't mind hunters in my woods, but all-terrain vehicles (ATVs) were a different story. Sportsmen today complain that more and more swaths of the state are being posted, and they're right—but I didn't see any other option. Before putting up my signs, though, I went around to my nearest neighbors and told them that despite the signs, they could hunt on my land anytime.

It was a futile gesture. I soon found out that those signs are powerful symbols in the backcountry. Telling neighbors they can hunt on your posted land defies local logic: if it's okay to hunt, why is the land posted? When rural Mainers detect a difference between what you say and what you do, they detect someone from the city.

3

One day in March, while cruising a stretch of my wetlands along a frozen back road, I noticed someone had cut two large red maples on my property. A couple trees more or less might go unnoticed, but these were the only trees of height along the edge of a low swampy area, and their absence transformed the landscape. It appeared to be the work of a vandal, not a logger: the stump cuts were sloppy, not neatly buzzed the way a pro with a powerful, well-maintained chainsaw would do it. And while the trunk sections had been hacked up and removed (no doubt for firewood), huge pieces of the crowns (called slash) had been left to rot along the road—a bush-league violation of state law.

Staring at the broken limbs and sawdust scattered across the snow, I felt like someone had robbed my house. I wondered what kind of person would so callously disregard property rights—in a region where property rights are held sacred—and then I noticed that the "No Trespassing" signs I had stapled to trees along the road were gone. Whoever cut those two maples had also ripped off all my signs.

I got into my truck and headed for home, thinking about what to do next. Call the state police? What could they do? Something told me that my neighbor Earl would know about this. The trees had been cut near my boundary with his land—or more accurately, his father Earl Sr.'s land. Earl Jr., a laborer in his early twenties, lived in a shingled shack on twenty-four acres owned by his dad, just half a mile down the road from me. I had met him more than a year ago, when he stopped by to warn me darkly about what he regarded as too much enthusiasm on the part of the local dog catcher. I hadn't seen him since, but I often see his flinching black mongrel slinking around my house early in the morning.

I could hear the dog barking inside as I turned into Earl Jr.'s driveway and parked next to a fleet of snowmobiles, most of them with hoods up and greasy parts spread across the snow. No one answered the door, and as I turned to leave I noticed the stack of freshly cut firewood on his porch. It was red maple and hadn't been split yet, so I could easily see that the cross section exactly matched one of the two new stumps on my property.

Back home I called my neighbor Judith to see if she knew about Earl Jr. and his chainsaw rampage. Like me, Judith is from away (England by way of Connecticut) and does not allow motorized vehicles on her land, which in her case constitutes some four hundred acres. Unlike me, she is rumored to be quite well off, although hand-to-mouth locals like Earl might regard the economic divide between Judith and myself as irrelevant, especially as Judith does not exactly parade her wealth.

It has occurred to me that a Marxist graduate student might find Judith's lifestyle too ascetic. A small, gray-haired woman with a PhD in something or other and a strict Christian

Scientist, Judith abhors waste of any kind. She's the leader of our town's conservation committee (which she roped me into joining), and she recycles used envelopes—not into the recycling bin, but as envelopes. She drinks no alcohol and eats no meat, wears sensible shoes and drives a vintage economy car that appears to be held together by eco-friendly bumper stickers. If she were younger, she would attend Phish concerts. At her age, she travels to solar energy seminars.

Among Judith's many endearing qualities is her valiant effort to appreciate the locals on their own terms, and I knew she could help with Earl. "Oh yes, Earl thought those signs were mine," she said, "and he came tearing up my driveway, blowing his horn, screaming about how I was posting his land and all. Said he'd give me one hour to remove the signs or he'd do it himself. I said I didn't know anything about it and he left. But he was so threatening, I called the state police. They came and took a report. Anyway, just before Christmas I stopped by his place with some cookies, hoping to mend things, and he was very apologetic. He said he knew it was you who put up the signs."

"Well, he hasn't come by to see me."

"Some people find it easier to yell at a woman. Anyway, he claims your land starts at the sofa."

"No, my land starts way before the sofa."

I don't know what made me sadder—the idea that a piece of living-room furniture dumped in my swamp had become a local landmark, or the fact that I was seriously discussing its relative significance as a boundary marker. It was one of the few times since moving to Maine that I wished I was back in an office in Rockefeller Center. "I've got a recorded survey of my line," I said defensively. "It's marked at the corner by a spike and was blazed through the woods years ago. In fact, that line goes back to King George." It was the truth: way before the sofa, my northern property edge was a section of what was called the Ballard Line—one of the original royal land grants that carved Maine into vast, exploitable tracts during the Colonial era.

"Well, you better talk to Earl."

"Do you have his number?"

"I don't think he has a phone, you'll have to go down there. I'd be careful; he flies off the handle. Here's the name of the state trooper who took the report. You might need it."

I put it off, and couldn't sleep that night. Coincidentally, in the course of writing an article for *This Old House* about picket fences, I had recently talked to a legal expert who told me that boundary disputes were *the leading cause of homicide between neighbors*. I twisted in the sheets as my range war escalated: Ballard Line . . . sofa . . . surveys . . . Hatfields . . . McCoys . . . shotguns. In the morning I calmly assessed the situation: I had a survey, he had an opinion. But I had a wife, small children, school committee meetings, and a 401-K; he had nonworking snowmobiles. It obviously wasn't worth getting angry about, but it would also be wrong to leave it unsettled. I decided to go down to Earl's on Saturday, when most people are in their best mood.

Again the dog barked but no one answered as I banged on Earl's door. This time as I turned to leave, a rusted Buick roared up the driveway. It was Earl's dad. I introduced myself and explained the situation, apologizing if I'd caused any confusion. Earl Sr., who clearly knew all about it, waved an arm dismissively and said "Nah, it's all taken care of. C'mon, get in, let's go take a look at that boundary."

Earl Sr. hadn't shaved in a few weeks, and a small blood stain ran down the silver whiskers on his right cheek. He told me he was 47, and as we bounced along the back road he carried on cheerfully about bastard loggers and son-of-a-bitch beaver poachers and goddamn trespassers. I could see where his son got his anger, but in the father it had become philosophical, mellowed with age. And he was trying to mend fences with me.

"See where that brook runs through my swamp?" he said, pointing out my window. "There's trout this big in there," and he held his hands two feet apart. "I don't tell too many people about it, 'cause I like to save 'em for the kids. You take your kids in there next summer."

We pulled up to the edge of my property. I showed him the spike in the ground, and the blazed trees. "Ayuh," he said. "That's the line."

"I was worried I had it wrong," I said, "because your son ripped my signs down all the way to the sofa."

"All taken care of."

"And these maples of mine he cut," I said, pointing to the slash. "He should know this is shoreland district."

"Well, that was probably my uncle the road commissioner cut those," said Earl Sr. as we got back in his car.

His uncle would have been Alfred, a good man with major sideburns who looks like a cross between Elvis and George

Jones. I knew Alfred would never leave slash along the roadside, nor would he have any reason to cut those trees. I wondered if Earl Sr. knew that his son had cut my trees, but I
decided not to mention the firewood on the porch. Better to
let new maples sprout from the stumps than to plant a seed
of hostility. If I read his dad right, Earl Jr. wouldn't be cutting
any more trees on my land.

4

The first Sunday of spring dawned clear, bright and reasonably warm, and I woke up early and excited. My anticipation had nothing to do with all the Maine-themed movies up for Oscars that night. The main attraction in these parts was a rite of spring called Maine Maple Sugar Sunday—although locals were grateful that Hollywood agreed to hold off its ceremony until the sugar shacks closed.

It was the first time in years that I did not have to attend the Oscars as a magazine editor, or even pretend to care. Instead, today I was on a mission: I needed to buy some used maple-sugaring equipment, and I figured the statewide open house of syrup producers was a good place to scavenge. While my kids were gorging on syrup and ice cream, I would be chatting up swarthy men of the woods while scanning their barns for neglected buckets and boilers.

When it came to sap equipment, my needs were simple. The loggers who deforested my land twenty years ago left fourteen old sugar maples along the road—enough to produce syrup for friends and family while enjoying the ritual of tapping trees and boiling down the sap in the outdoor brick oven I planned to build. But because forty gallons of maple sap boil down to just one gallon of syrup, the essential piece of equipment is a fireproof container large enough to hold massive quantities of the clear, watery tree sap. A stock pot won't do: You want something wide and shallow, to speed the evaporation process. You want something made of steel, about three by four feet. And if you're like me, you want something under one hundred dollars.

What Earland Luce wanted was a bigger sap operation. Earland, whom I discovered that afternoon, runs a maple syrup farm some twelve miles from my house. A few years back he invested in a professional, stainless steel sap cooker roughly the size of an Airstream trailer. Although heated solely by wood, the gleaming unit in his sugar shack appeared ready to blast off. Pipes channeled raw sap into several giant vats, where hundreds of gallons boiled away furiously as massive ducts funneled steam and wood smoke up through the rafters. Earland, the Captain Nemo of this gurgling vessel, was wrapped in a foot-long beard and a sticky apron. He ricocheted around the shack, stoking the fire, skimming scum, pouring off syrup, and changing filters.

I was taking in this activity when I caught sight of Earland's *old* sap operation: a three-by-four steel sap pan, balancing on rafters directly over my head.

"Say, you still use that old sap pan?" I asked him.

"*No.*" Making maple syrup is a process of reduction, and Earland had extended the principle to the English language.

"Would you be willing to sell it?"

"*Yes.*"

"How much?"

"*Reasonable.*"

"Fifty dollars?"

"*Sold.*"

I wish he had hesitated even briefly, instead of leaving me with the nagging suspicion I could have had it for thirty, but the gavel had come down, as it were.

Early next Thursday morning I arrived in my truck to pick up the pan, and the dawn's calm was pierced by the unmistakable sound of a violent domestic squabble. Earland, so few of words the other day, had apparently tripled his vocabulary—and his angry howling made me fear for his wife's safety. I stood outside the house wondering if I should go home and call the sheriff when Earland walked out of the barn, water bucket in hand. "You miserable old hay-burner!" he shouted back at his ox. Relieved that Earland was directing his verbal tirade at a half-ton beast of burden, I greeted him warmly and we fell into chatting as he went about his chores, watering and denigrating the other livestock.

"Sap run's just about over," he said. "Now comes the hard part. Got over five hundred buckets to scrub clean—but this year I've got a little more help than I expected," he added solicitously, with exaggerated enunciation on "lit-tle."

"How's that?" I played along.

"Caught me some teenagers messin' around with somethin' what wasn't theirs, is what. The first time they come around my woods and dumped my sap buckets in the river, I didn't catch 'em. But the second time, they come right after a snow. Dumb-ass kids. So I got the sheriff and we followed the tracks right to their house. Caught three of 'em."

"What did you do?"

"Well, this one kid's mother said her husband died last year and she had no money and all. So the sheriff says to me, 'You wanna press charges or have 'em work it off?' And I said 'They can work it off, but it's gonna be on *my* terms. I figure fifty dollars in equipment lost, plus fifty dollars for my time. I pay one dollar an hour, no more.'"

Earland's gavel had come down again. But he wasn't finished: "One of them kids started in to doin' this"—Earland rolled his eyes around in his head—"and I said 'Hold on there just one minute, sonny! When I'm talkin' to you, I expect you to look me *straight* in the eye! You keep up that attitude and you'll wind up in the Crowbar Hotel.'" He was referring to the famously decrepit state prison in Thomaston, the inspiration for Stephen King's *Shawshank Redemption*, since torn down. "'And they pay even less than I do.'"

The steel pan was heavy and it took both of us to heft it into the back of my small truck, which sagged under the weight. I may have paid too much for it, I thought as I drove home, but I got to meet Earland, and I didn't have to work fifty hours for it.

5

Maine isn't the only place where fires are deliberately set in the spring to control weeds, rejuvenate soil, and clear brush. But it could be the only place left where burning constitutes a cultural activity. Around here, burning brings families and sometimes whole communities together, as I learned when I endeavored to torch my seven acres of blueberry land.

I also found out how hard it is to start a fire when you want one—and how quickly a fire that finally gets going can rage out of control. Nature has its own controls to prevent fires from starting too easily; breach them and, to paraphrase Dante, risk entering the theme park from hell. For that, you don't have to go to out West, where wildfires destroy hundreds of thousands of acres, or even Orlando. Live in rural Maine long enough and you'll have your own experience with scary fires.

My blueberry field hadn't been burned in years, so it was due. I knew that because locals told me so, and also because last summer's crop was so choked with weeds that my blueberry rakes could hardly get through the tangled mass; I had to leave most of the fruit for the wild turkeys, who didn't mind the weeds or the mosquitoes.

Weeds could be cut with a mower, but blueberries just

seem to do better after a fire. It's a form of pruning that defies logic: the berries thrive in highly acidic soil (provided by centuries of decomposed evergreen forest), yet burning creates ash, which is alkaline. I believe the real reason Mainers burn their fields is that guys love starting really cool fires.

No one appreciates a good fire more than a fireman, so when it came time to burn my field, I rang up Tom, the chief of our local volunteer fire department. Over the years I would come to appreciate Tom as being exactly the sort of person you want in a fire chief: even-tempered, well respected (in part because he is so respectful of others), and unlikely to lose control—of himself or a raging chimney fire. Fires generate plenty of panic to go around, and somebody has to keep his cool. Tom's your man.

"Hmmm, we could probably help you out," said Tom. "Be good training for the men in controlling brush fires. I'll get back to you."

In rural New England that means "we'll show up when you've completely forgotten about it and are not in the least expecting us." Actually, I got eight hours notice. Tom drove up one Monday morning a few weeks later and said "We're coming tonight, five o'clock."

Volunteer fire departments across rural America are struggling with serious manpower shortages, but you wouldn't know it from the turnout at my farm that night. More than a dozen cars streamed into our two gravel driveways (not counting all the friends and relatives who showed up to watch the inferno), followed by the town's pair of aging fire trucks. If the TV show *Green Acres* had a S.W.A.T. team, it could have been cast by my local fire department. There was Jeff from the hardware store, and Wesley the town selectman (who reminded me to get down to the town office and be sworn in as the newest member of the conservation committee), and just a bunch of Other Guys you see around town all the time—but tonight they were different. Tonight they had big reflective hats, and huge boots with brass buckles, and five-gallon backpack water tanks that made them look like spacemen even if some of the tanks had leaks that dribbled water down into their butt cracks, which were generally visible. They were men on a mission. My eight-year-old's lower jaw was on the floor.

"Usually we burn a fire break around the edge, and then light the center and just let it go," explained Tom. "You care about that picnic table? Just kidding."

To get things going, one of the firemen carried a drop torch, which is like a watering can with a flaming nozzle that pours drops of lit kerosene onto the field. The other firemen with their water packs and shovels fanned out across the land, and the burning began.

Slowly, it turned out. The air was damp and heavy, and the brush was already greening. The fire burned wherever the drop torch had been, but it wasn't spreading much. After two hours, with darkness looming, Tom called it a night and said "it's a little spotty in places." I thanked him and handed over a three hundred dollar donation to the fire department.

The next morning I went out and looked at the "spot" that hadn't burned. It was big enough to be taxed. It was most of my field. I called Tom, who said it wouldn't be a problem for me to torch the rest of it myself. The fire break his men burned had left a barren perimeter, so any fire in the center wouldn't spread to my surrounding woods.

Fine, but I needed help, and I knew where to get it. My brother-in-law Matt, who was born in Korea, is a professional teppan-yaki chef—a caterer who specializes in the style of Japanese cooking over searingly hot fires. He loves a good flame, but he grew up in Iowa where people don't burn their fields. "Wow, we get to set something on fire and not get into trouble? What time?"

It was a bright, calm Saturday afternoon—great for sunburn but not so good for brush burning. Gallons of gasoline flared like napalm strikes wherever we poured, but with no wind the fire barely moved. (I found out later that kerosene works better and is less dangerous because it's not explosive.) Finally we spread out some hay bales and managed to get most of the field charred enough to match our faces. Matt had the field under control, so I went off to burn an unsightly pile of old lumber that had been ripped out of our house during the renovation. This pile was pretty close to my woods, but I didn't think much about it, having spent an entire day watching fire refuse to burn. I torched the pile and stood back.

Then I stood back further. And further. Lumber drying for decades in a farmhouse, I realized, is not the same as a field of green bushes. Suddenly I had a bonfire that towered into the sky. Then I looked at the ground. The pile rested on an old hayfield—and the hay, although green, was igniting around the inferno like the map on the opening credits of

Bonanza. It was spreading fast toward my woods. I was wearing my backpack sprayer, but it made a tiny jet of water compared to the deafening inferno, and as soon as I doused one area, another started up again. I could feel my already sunburned arms and face blistering as I moved in closer to fight the flames. I was starting to panic as I yelled for Matt. "Get the hose!" I shouted. That took many more minutes because I stupidly hadn't hooked up the several hundred feet of garden hose needed to reach the fire.

The flames were about ten feet from my woods when we finally got things under control. By the time we called it a day, my field was still full of brush too green to burn—I'd have to mow it—and it was still a little spotty, as was I. But my forest, thank God, wasn't spotty at all. Fire becomes dangerous when you stop fearing it, I learned. Recently I heard that Maine's commercial blueberry growers are moving away from fire, in favor of weedkill sprays. I won't spray my berries, but I stopped burning and switched to mowing every other year. Someday I'll probably burn that field again, but not until that fire stops burning in my brain.

6

For several years I contributed regular articles to *TV Guide* from Maine without watching television, which entertained me greatly—at least, considerably more than TV itself ever has. One day an editor from the magazine called with some breaking news: the Pets.com sock puppet (a TV commercial character, as I soon learned) was suing Triumph (an obscene sock dog on the Conan O'Brien show, I discovered) for slander and trade infringement. The editor needed a full report by Friday. "What is Pets.com?" I asked him. "And who is Triumph?"

"What are you, living under a rock?" he replied incredulously.

Well, in a manner of speaking, yes. I'd recently removed several Paleozoic schists from my kitchen garden using an ingenious system of plank levers, boulder counterweights, and a cursing wife. It's the same technique employed by the ancient Egyptians (who also married their slaves) to build the pyramids. Farming in Maine is essentially mining—and neither occupation rates high on any magazine's list of desirable jobs (not to mention desirable husbands).

So it's a reasonable question to ask why someone with a college education, a job in national journalism, and an expense account would chuck it all for the company of flesh-eating blackflies and a life of back-breaking labor in a rocky field.

It's certainly a question my businessman father has asked; my bank had a similar query (in triplicate, notarized) when I applied for the mortgage on my farm. But mostly it's a question I ask myself—usually when bent over a hoe as rivulets of sweat sting my eyeballs.

I suppose I farm because there is beer, which never tastes better than after a day in the field. In that sense, farming gives me something to look forward to on a daily basis—as opposed to the seasonal anticipation of real tomatoes in August. I know very good farmers who drink only tea. I respect them, but I don't understand them.

I farm because the next seven million dollar T. Rex could be anywhere. If I find it under my hoe, I promise not to name him Sue.

I farm because it gives me something to do instead of write, and all writers need that. Like fields, pages must sometimes lay fallow; filling a page too soon can be as foolhardy as transplanting melons in May, which was my first mistake this cold, rainy spring. Now, from my desk where I look out over lush fields, blooming gardens and shriveled melon seedlings, I wait for the moment when weeds come faster than words, and I'm out the door, hoe happily in hand.

I farm in revolt against the grocery store, where checkout clerks don't know what parsley is, or where French fries come from. I may break down and buy a few melons at the supermarket this summer, but that's about all I'll be squeezing in the produce section. Even the large organic sections of good supermarkets feature the same bland, perfectly shaped varieties of fruits and vegetables—the ones that travel well and look uniformly green, or red, or yellow, as the case may be. Free of pesticides, they are, but also of flavor. One roams the aisles in vain for a purple winter storage apple called Black Oxford (an early Maine variety I'm grafting in my orchard), or the crook-necked canning tomato Gilbertie Paste, a rare Connecticut heirloom I've planted this year. I farm because I want to try them all, even though there aren't enough summers in my life.

Yet when you think about it, Americans lost their connection to the land in the span of just a few summers. The industrialization of food in America was a direct result of World War II, which in that sense we lost. I'm not being trivial: in 1945 (according to census and USDA surveys) one fifth of all Americans still *lived* on farms; many more worked in agriculture, and most others still cracked fresh local eggs, drank milk from a nearby farmer and had at least one family member who cooked real meals every day. Besides rapid urbanization, the war brought canned food, frozen food, fast food, high-speed truck transport, hybrid seeds, and agribusiness. By 1991, only two percent of Americans called their home a farm. Today, farms are food factories, the actual labor performed by migrants who have no permanent home, much less a white clapboard Cape and a big red barn.

Well-meaning city dwellers fret about the plight of today's farm laborers, but they don't for a minute imagine that farming could be something noble. Farm work is the nadir of drudgery—the lowest rung on the Darwinian ladder above crevice dwelling—something to be regulated, unionized, watched carefully for foul-ups. Smart people, on the other hand, go to college and perform important (non-union) tasks for big corporations in offices. After work—no hay to rake or beans to thresh—they go to gyms and climb stair machines.

Farmers also go to college these days. The nation's agricultural schools, supported heavily by agribusiness, teach them how to be profitable. (Lesson One: grow genetically engineered Red Russet potatoes for McDonald's.) They might even teach you when to plant melons in Maine. But they won't teach your boy how to play kickball in the orchard without knocking flowers off the apple trees, and there's no textbook on how to hose out the sheep shed without disturbing the robin's nest.

I farm for that way of life.

I also live in the 21st century. So even though I don't inhabit the real world of battling TV sock puppets, I was able to get the gist of their globe-shattering conflict with a few phone calls, and I filed the story on deadline. America got the scoop; the Republic survived. Here in the backcountry, real life goes on. The garden grows, the beer is cold, the summer people have arrived.

7

I 've come to notice that summer people shop differently than locals. For one thing, people from away actually buy stuff. Locals never buy anything that isn't a necessity. They might sit around the store all day, talking about buying something, but as the actual act of purchasing requires money, not much else happens. It's amazing how many tourists will fly in and out of a store here, dipping enthusiastically into their wallets, while the same old-timer is still sitting there, just getting warmed up to begin talking about buying something that you know he won't buy all summer. He's in no hurry.

Not like the summer folk, who are always in a hurry even when they're on vacation. They do, however, take time to lock their shiny cars and turn on the alarms. Car theft is nonexistent in these parts—if you wanted to steal a valuable vehicle you'd take a tractor, most of which have keys rusted into the ignition, and no alarms of any kind—but the tourists aren't taking any chances.

Tourists also seem to know exactly what they want to buy—and they must have it. Some of them actually say "I must have that!," which is probably how they got so much stuff, and why they have to work so hard and always be in a hurry. They also take the customer/merchant roles seriously;

they expect deference from shopkeepers, which they don't get from Elmer.

Elmer's Barn is a local institution and a junk store of national renown, if such a thing is possible. I've met people in New York who swoon over the mention of this rickety Route 17 emporium and its welcoming signpost:

KEEP DOGS IN CAR
NO SHIT

The message works on just about every level you can think of, and while I doubt Elmer was personally inspired by haiku, I often reflect on the peculiar Zen of my purchases there. I've been buying dusty stuff from Elmer since I lived in several big cities. I carted chairs from Elmer down to an apartment in Brooklyn, moved them to Los Angeles and back to New York. Now they are in my farmhouse, eight miles from where I bought them 15 years ago, which is the Maine version of karma, I suppose. Among the hundreds of things I have bought from Elmer are an antique copper sink now in my pantry (sixty dollars) and a gasoline-powered blueberry win-nower (one hundred twenty-five dollars).

Elmer himself (few people know that he has a last name, which is Wilson) is a mountainous man who nevertheless manages to hide in plain sight behind all the junk. He claims to be descended from horse traders, and he loves bargaining. But he also knows that his asking prices are far below what the fancier antique shops charge, even in Maine. Yes, you have to paw through lots of junk. But in the jungle world of junk dealers, Elmer is in fact rather selective. He loves cool old farm stuff and recently bought an abandoned sawmill up the road, with the intention of renovating it. Elmer doesn't do anything fast, though, so I don't expect to see Elmer's Lumber Barn anytime soon.

He's got better things to do, like writing a brochure with tips to make your visit more enjoyable. For example, the first page says "Children Welcome! NOT LIABLE FOR ANY ACCIDENTS OR INJURIES (not a daycare center)."

Most injuries are suffered to customer's egos. One day a neatly pressed guy from Massachusetts (according to his Volvo plate) stopped in and inquired, "How much for those two carved lions in the yard?"

"Six thousand dollars," said Elmer.

"How much for one?"

"Sixty-five hundred," Elmer replied without cracking a smile.

The Volvo guy stood silently, processing, for a few minutes. He didn't get it. He didn't make the expected joking repast, like "I'd hate to hear what the head costs."

"Youse a little slow, ain't ya?" Elmer eventually said, finally cracking a smile.

That wasn't how Mr. Massachusetts was accustomed to being treated by a shop owner. He swiveled and marched out the door, ears pinned to his head. Elmer just shrugged at me, pointed to a sign on the wall and said "I guess he didn't read it."

The sign said:

ALL PRICES SUBJECT TO
CUSTOMER ATTITUDE

Another of my favorite local shopkeepers is Ken Spahr, who runs an antique stove and lamp store down the road from Elmer. Ken is an old graybeard way beyond retirement age, but he putters around in his shop, surrounded by mountains of cast iron stove parts and vats of lye, extolling the virtues of The Good Old Days When Stuff Was Made Right to anyone who will listen.

Ken has been helping me renovate the old door hardware in my house, and I always leave his shop feeling embarrassed by my metallurgical inadequacies. He's from the *Popular Mechanics* generation, when it was assumed that all real men had metal shops in their cellar. "How anyone can *live* without a belt grinder is beyond me," he once said in total seriousness. But I also leave his shop feeling able to fix a lot more stuff around the house.

Ken loves to tell the story of how he lost his finger using a joiner, a power tool that can instantly shave layers off wood (or anything else). "I drove myself to the hospital and told them what happened. The nurse said 'Did you bring in the finger?'"

At this point in the story Ken starts laughing and shaking his head. "I told her, 'Honey, I guess you don't know what a joiner does.'" He laments the general ignorance of the populace, but if everyone knew what a joiner does, Ken would lose his purpose.

One day I told Ken how I was having a hard time getting propane delivered for my antique wood-and-gas kitchen cookstove. (There is no natural gas utility in Maine; if you want a gas appliance you're stuck with propane delivery.) My

1926 cast-iron stove features a two-burner wood compart-
ment (also suitable for coal), next to four gas burners. It was
a hybrid introduced around the time when Americans were
switching to gas but didn't quite feel comfortable giving up
the old reliable fuels of wood and coal. We like it because it
combines the obvious convenience of gas with the ambiance
of burning real wood in winter.

Wood-and-gas stoves are still technically legal here, but
propane suppliers don't like them because it seems inherently
dicey to have red-hot cinders glowing a few inches from a gas
line—especially a "match-light" stove, which means it has no
pilot lights. So it's hard to find a company that will deliver
propane.

"My mother had one of those stoves," said Ken. "It was
great. Sure, every now and then she'd blow the doors off the
house, but who gives a shit?" Then Ken shook his head in
disgust and railed against lawyers, energy companies, and the
government, concluding: "These days nobody feels comfortable unless they've got a finger up their ass."

It's not quite how (or where) I would have put it, but I
understood the sentiment. Those cranky summer visitors
rushing in and out of the stores and spending too much
money do seem to have misplaced a digit somewhere—which
is probably why they can't just set a spell. On the other hand,
I don't care to lose a finger in a joiner either. I admit there are
days this summer when I walk into Elmer's in my mud-
streaked Tingley boots and greasy dungarees, looking for a
zinc hinge pin, and those beautiful summer people shopping
for slate sinks seem like a tantalizing dream.

Lately I spend less and less time at Elmer's. After five years in Maine I feel I've accumulated enough dusty old stuff, and I'm reluctant to spend more money. I guess in that sense I'm becoming more like the locals. Not that I'm totally in synch with them: If I ever spent a whole morning hanging around Elmer's Barn, I'd be pissed at myself for wasting so much time. So I exist in my own world, neither here nor there—disconnected from the tourists who recall my previous life, yet not really able to let go and just hang out with the locals. I stay home a lot.

8

The town library posted a notice reporting several recent home robberies, an unusual and disappointing trend here. To country folk, crime is like the Republican Convention—scary but far away, in an alternate universe where people are forced to wear uncomfortable shoes. And yet if burglars must burgle, posting their deeds in the library is at least reassuringly rural.

Rural or not, the bad news prompted an assessment of my valuables for insurance purposes, so I've been thinking about all the stuff I have, and what might attract a thief.

If the line of boat trailers down at the pond landing on Saturday mornings is any indication, a burglar in these parts would probably head straight for my fishing gear. He could keep my thirty-nine dollar Abu Garcia Accu Balance rod-and reel from Sam's Club, so long as he doesn't mess with my Lazy Ike, which is irreplaceable. The Lazy Ike is a curved wooden lure about three inches long with two sets of treble hooks. It's spray-painted in a black-and-white mottled motif and wiggles through the water in a funny sidewinder way. It's interesting as a piece of wood, but it doesn't look like or act like anything in nature; when my father-in-law first saw it, he didn't say "If I was a bass, I'd eat that," like he does with the more realistic lures costing ten dollars down at Hussey's General Store.

But Lazy Ike has two main advantages. First, he was free: I pulled him out of a tree along a river in Michigan with a pair of pliers on my dad's boat. Second, he catches lots of bass, more than any lure I've ever had—except for the Rattlin' Chug Bug, which I also found but lost. I've lost Lazy Ike several times while fishing in my canoe, but I always manage to paddle over and extract him from the lily pads or the tree stump. I don't so much like Ike as love him, and he's with me long-term. Thieves will be prosecuted to the fullest extent.

I should probably put Sarah's butter churn in a safe place too. It's a nice old glass "Dazey" model, the kind that turns half a gallon of cream into a big glob of fresh butter (we've never measured how much) after about twenty minutes of cranking. The Lehman's non-electric catalog sells reproductions for one hundred twenty-nine dollars, but this is the real thing. Some people would say it's a lot of work for butter, and in fact there isn't much point if you're using grocery-store cream. But if you've got fresh farm cream, as people in these parts do, you can make the best butter you've ever tasted, dark yellow and smelling like clover as it melts and sizzles in a fry pan.

Pet theft is a growing problem everywhere in America. In our house that could mean loss of my kids' beloved pet cocoon, Mark McGwire. Captured and jarred as a caterpillar a few weeks ago, Mark is scheduled to become a Monarch butterfly soon. He lived in apparent comfort on a diet of milkweed leaves until one day when he suddenly became a bright green pod, dangling from the perforated lid of the Mason jar. I don't know why my Red Sox-addicted kids would name a caterpillar after a National League player. Nor do I know why our butterfly will travel from our dining room table to the Amazon jungle in the next few months, assuming no thief finds him first.

A fashion-conscious crook wouldn't find much in the wardrobe department around here, but we do have some valuable raw material. Sarah, who spins wool, recently acquired an entire sheep's fleece. Matted and stained with dung, it's nothing you'd snuggle up to on a winter night just yet. First you have to sort it, discarding the short fibers and the parts that won't come clean. Then you need to hand wash and rinse it. If the rinse water isn't exactly the same temperature as the wash water, the fleece will felt and be useless for spinning. Then you card it, which involves pulling the wool through a pair of fine wire brushes to align all the fibers. That gives you rolags, which are ready to be spun into yarn—a process that takes both time and skill. Only then, assuming you know how to knit or weave, can you make something warm to wear out of a sheep fleece.

I can't believe we don't bring our tire swing in every night. A good tire swing is hard to find, although location is admittedly part of the appeal. You want a nice supple old tire that bends when you sit on it. Then you want to drill a hole through the bottom to drain water. I don't know how long a tire of some sort has been hanging from the two-hundred-year-old red oak in our front yard, but a foot-thick branch has grown completely around the rope, and I'm sure grass hasn't grown under that spot since the Truman Administration. When our tree finally dies, the tire will no doubt go to a museum, which will sell reproduction earrings in the gift shop.

Writing about these prized possessions is risky, I realize. In these parts, everybody knows where everybody lives. (Our mail service goes by names more than addresses.) Country life has given me new appreciation for things like fishing lures and butter churns, but it's also made me love stuff less—even good stuff like this. If I was a bass, I'd eat Lazy Ike—and sooner or later some lunker will do just that, right before he wraps the line around a stump and snaps it off.

Reborn
in a Barn

(The Second Year)

9

Since quitting my day job and moving to Maine, I no longer attend the Cannes Film Festival. Instead, I go to county fairs in Union and Windsor—the best places around here to see purple hair and navel rings, if that's what you're looking for. An agricultural fair, with its tractor displays and dusty poultry halls, is a world away from the alleged glamor of the French Riviera (where you can see purple hair and nipple rings, if that's what you're looking for), and I can't say a stroll down the Windsor Fairgrounds' Beano Boulevard transported me back to the Rue d'Antibes. Still, a Maine fair has more in common with the cinematic circus that greeted me every year on the C'te d'Azur than you might imagine.

Film festival and Maine fair both feature bewildering and overlapping event schedules that are invariably wrong. Both are administered by impenetrable commissions whose representatives communicate using the international sign language of the bureaucrat—the shrugged shoulder. Both are good places to lose your wallet at night. Both lure rubes into vast halls of wagering where the odds are stacked tremendously in favor of the house. Both transform quiet communities into chattering linguistic Babels, where strangers from exotic places like Burkina Faso (Cannes) or Rhode Island (Maine fair) mingle with wide-eyed locals. Finally, both feature over-priced food whose principal ingredient is the French fry.

Nowhere is that delicacy more celebrated than at the Windsor Fair, where the potato schools include Old Orchard Beach Style, Lady Tish's, Kevin's, Patti's, Bob's Famous, Mr. C's, Fresh Cut, and World's Greatest. Yes, the French fry connoisseur enters another world at Windsor—a world that includes Reggie's World of Sausage and his can-you-top-this competitor across the midway, Bacon Dogs.

Maine fairs also elevate the indigenous cuisine—best represented by that Yankee staple, fried dough. A masterpiece of function over form, fried dough is essentially a doughnut without all the bother of shaping. It's the same noble do-it-yourself aesthetic that informs everything from barn building to alewife netting in rural Maine. At the Union Fair I ran into my friend Mark Hannibal, who owns a local restaurant, and he mentioned his own kids' addiction to fried dough. "Every year after the fair, we try to make it at the restaurant, but it never comes out right," he confessed.

"Have you tried letting your grease get really old and rancid?"

But he was already gone, towed through the crowd by youngsters to the looming Witch Castle. My family followed his, where we joined a throng of fidgeting grade schoolers watching the operator attempt to repair one of the ride's cars. His diagnostic test, which involved repeatedly striking the undercarriage with a claw hammer while cursing in pentameter, confirmed my suspicion that carnival technicians do not take core studies at MIT, much less Harvard Divinity.

And the booming economy makes these rides even scarier; workers are hard to find ("Help Wanted" signs papered the Union Fair), and potentially deadly amusements like the Pharaoh's Fury and the Skymaster appeared to be operated by runaways.

Tired of the noise and filth of the Union midway, I left the kids at home when I ventured to the Windsor Fair a week later in search of livestock displays, and was glad I did: There again were the Pharaoh's Fury, the Skymaster, the same glassy-eyed operators. I shivered and headed for the farm museum.

Here I was in my element. Keep your fried dough, just give me a dank barn full of corn binders, potato diggers, and manure spreaders. I suppose today's purple-haired visitors are expected to wonder in awe how people ever used these primitive wooden tools, but I found myself wishing I had them on my own farm today.

Of course I would need some draft animals to pull them, so my next stop was the livestock arena. Strangely enough it was there on the sagging bleachers, while watching the judges rule on Junior Yearling Heifers, that I first felt as if I were back in Cannes. This absurd competition, in which way-too-serious teenagers (no purple hair here) used metal gaffs to pull cows' feet into formation for the inspection of ribbon-wielding experts, reminded me of the equally ridiculous film competitions I'd seen at festivals from Cannes to Berlin to Venice and the Oscars. The golden palms, lions, and bears handed out at these media frenzies are all golden calves—and while I've never been a huge fan of Woody

Allen, I've always admired his refusal to participate in artistic competitions.

Driving home, I felt relieved to be out of the arena, so to speak, and able to enjoy a movie, or a heifer, on its own terms without considering its relative merits. I also felt a seasonal grief, as the Windsor Fair marks the unofficial end of summer around here. It was getting to be time to stack wood.

10

My Uncle Bill, an aircraft historian, was involved a few years ago in the search for a French plane that may have crashed near Calais, Maine in 1927, several weeks before Lindbergh's historic flight across the Atlantic. The biplane and its two pilots left Paris hoping to beat Lindy as the first across the pond (going the other way), but their plane disappeared, presumably into the ocean. Yet accounts by old-timers in the woods around Calais suggested the French might have made land, albeit at terminal velocity; a hermit (that's actually how he's described) named Anson Berry heard a plane pass low through dense fog over his cabin that night—at a time when air travel was rare indeed. Because the wooden craft was largely biodegradable (alas, ahead of its time in more ways than one), the searchers' main hope was to locate its massive engine.

"They'll never find it," announced my father-in-law when he heard about the plan over dinner one night. "Some woodsman dragged that thing out of the forest a long time ago. It's probably rigged up to a saw in his barn right now, bucking up firewood—and he's sure as shit not gonna talk about it to some history buffs in Gore-Tex boots."

Well, that tells you about my father-in-law, not to mention volumes about backwoods Maine—the hermit named

Anson, the windfall in the woods, a crafty old Yankee with a monkey wrench and a fear of flatlanders—enough Puritan themes to constitute a literary movement, all from a plane out of Paris. It also says a lot about the rural Mainer's obsession with firewood (what else would you do with a French airplane engine?)—which is what reminded me of the story at the end of this cold, wet summer, while stacking wood against another impending winter.

I came late to the firewood aesthetic, having grown up in a suburban house with no fireplace at all. In fact, the heat of my boyhood was seemingly involuntary; I vaguely recall a heating appliance in the cellar but don't know what fueled it, nor do I recall ever hearing a single discussion about it. The first time I ever thought much about heat was in 1983, when Sarah and I rented our first apartment in Brooklyn. Heat there became a constant concern from November to March because there was none, and because the ancient radiators clanged and banged all night—waking you up to remind you that there was none.

Since then I have taken control of my life in many ways, the procurement of heat being one. Last year at a cost of seven thousand dollars I installed a new boiler and radiant-floor heat in my farmhouse. The system requires copious amounts of fossil fuel, of course, for which OPEC and its local distributors may decide to charge me another seven thousand dollars this winter. But I also have three woodstoves (one of which doubles as a kitchen cookstove) and several cords of seasoned firewood. So there.

Except it isn't that simple. Like most things today, wood

has gotten more complicated. Start with chimneys; my house has two very old brick ones. When my contractor George first saw them he said "You're not planning to use those, are you?"

"Well, actually . . . "

"Don't burn wood in unlined chimneys. You'll burn your house down," George said.

"Unlined?"

"Those old chimneys were held together with lime mortar, which degrades over time. Probably all sorts of holes up in there. One spark gets through and it's all over. You need to have them relined with new flues."

He was right, of course. George was an old family friend who had long ago escaped the fast lane—quitting his job as a precious metals trader on Wall Street to follow his dream of building houses in Maine. I knew I could trust him. Out went five thousand dollars for new chimney flues. And if you care about not spewing tons of particulate pollution into the air, you'll want one of the latest woodstoves with catalytic converters that re-burn smoke. I felt extravagant spending two thousand dollars for a woodstove until I met a woman in Bangor who spent twenty thousand dollars on a custom-made, ten-thousand-pound masonry woodstove for her kitchen. (You can spend more, she assured me.)

Then comes the wood—and it comes unstacked, by the way, a mountain of timber, dust, bugs, fungus, and snakes dumped in the middle of your driveway. Need to get your car out? Get stacking. Wood heats you twice, goes the old saw, once when you chop it and once when you burn it. But you can get your blood downright boiling just stacking wood that somebody else chopped and split, believe me. A cord of seasoned hardwood weighs two tons; each stick weighs about five pounds. Two cords, five into eight thousand, carry over the three . . . (these are the things you think about while stacking wood) makes sixteen hundred pieces of wood. Bend, grab, straighten, stack ("chink"), bend, grab, straighten, stack ("chink") . . . sixteen hundred times. I ask my eight-year-old to help; he refuses. Should I take him out to the woodshed? By the end of the day you feel like you've stacked a woods, not some wood.

And written another check for the privilege. My firewood this year cost a pricey one hundred seventy-five dollars per cord, and the delivery guy said I should get it while I could at that level. Demand is high thanks in part to spiking heating oil prices, he said—but more to the point is the high cost of diesel fuel, which of course runs the trucks that bring the wood from upcountry. So that's the bottom line: there's no escaping OPEC, unless you chop your own wood in your own woods.

Which is what the previous owners of my property did. But from the neatly stacked piles of cut firewood I still see on walks through my woods, I suspect they got tired of all the bother, and turned up the thermostat. Now their abandoned woodpiles, like that French biplane, lie rotting into the forest floor. My Uncle Bill died during the summer of 2000 at age eighty; nothing of the airplane has been found.

11

The propellers whined as the Saab 340 banked over Yankee Stadium, lowering toward the Hudson for a morning cruise down the length of Manhattan. Cross-town streets fanned past like fence pickets before we pivoted over the Statue of Liberty's torch and across Brooklyn to a southwest landing at LaGuardia. When I first started flying between New York and Portland twenty years ago, the planes were full-size jets. Now both cities are bigger, richer and glitzier than ever—and the planes are puddle jumpers made by car companies. I'm sure that says more about the wretched state of air travel than anything about Manhattan and Maine, but the tiny low-flying planes do make for spectacular arrivals.

The excitement ended when we touched down and sat on the tarmac for thirty minutes—half as long as the flight itself—waiting for a gate. I was back in New York, on assignment from *Reader's Digest*, writing about an eighty-nine-year-old woman who rescued nearly a thousand Jews from Europe during World War II. She was in Manhattan, but my heart was in Queens and the Bronx: the city was in a frenzy over the subway series championship between baseball's richest team and its third-richest team.

In truth I was annoyed that a subway series never happened

during the years I lived there, when Sarah and I would annually cheer for the Mets and hiss at the Yankees (we were New Englanders even then). So on Thursday I wandered down to Great Jones Café, a Mets stronghold in the East Village, and watched my guys flame out. At least I didn't have to listen to any whooping Yankee obnoctoids. There was enough idiocy on the screen, as Mets fans cheered on their catcher, Mike Piazza, with signs like HE DELIVERS and PIAZZA DELIVERY ZONE. "*Piazza* means *plaza*!" I wanted to scream. "Place! Square! Courtyard! There is no cheese on it!"

In search of higher culture, I ambled down to a nearby jazz club where the last set of the Mingus Big Band was about to start. This was the fourteen-piece unit that Charles Mingus' widow put together, to keep his music alive after his death from Lou Gehrig's Disease in 1979. Using charts written by the arranger Sy Johnson, who worked with Mingus in the late seventies, the band swung through an hour's worth of Mingus standards, closing with the classic "Nostalgia in Times Square."

The music was great, like nothing in Maine—and I was feeling fairly nostalgic myself about New York at that point, although not enough to consider a stroll through Times Square. I couldn't recall the last time I had shoes on at two in the morning, and I flopped exhausted into a taxi for my hotel.

The next day was less romantic. At magazine offices around town, friends who work in cubicles until late at night ("gotta go, we're closing the book") talked earnestly about media mergers and masthead shuffles. None of it would mean anything to folks where I live now—even if it were about a significant publication like *Field & Stream*. And always came the inevitable talk of housing, the New Yorker's obsession.

"Remember those studio apartments in the East Village with the bathtub in the living room?" said a friend.

"How could I forget?" I replied. "You put a board over the tub and there's your dining-room table. With a shared toilet down the hall, right?"

"Right, like a youth hostel. Those are going for eighteen hundred a month."

"That's about half what you'd have to pay me to live there," I said. But there was a time when I actually wanted to live in New York badly enough to sell myself into that kind of slavery. Now I felt like Elliott Merrick, the New York author of the 1930s who moved to Vermont and described a return to Gotham in *Green Mountain Farm*: "Here are the lost city millions who can never be freed because they don't want to be freed."

Which is a good thing if you live in a quiet corner of the woods that you hope stays that way. With the airlines doing their part to keep people away, I felt safe in my solitude, if not downright smug.

Until I got home on Saturday afternoon. "I think we need to rent an apartment in town," said Sarah when I walked in the door.

"Huh?"

"The distance is really starting to get to me." Sarah was now teaching at the Ashwood Waldorf School in Camden that our kids attend, more than twenty miles from our farm. "It isn't just the driving," she went on. "I don't feel like I'm part of the school community way out here. I need to be closer."

She was finally putting words to one of our biggest fears— a major issue that until now we had danced around delicately. The fact is, our house is more isolated than we'd ever imagined. And it's a bigger problem for Sarah, who needs the kinship of friends much more than I. "We could get a place in town during the week, and stay out here on weekends."

"Camden's expensive," I said, which sounded absurd after hearing about Manhattan's eighteen-hundred-dollar-a-month hovels. "But we can look around."

Then came the details. We'd need another computer. What about my work phone? (Maybe I need to rent an office.) What about the dog? The cat? So much for getting a flock of sheep . . . Suddenly it all seemed hugely complicated and limiting, the opposite of why we moved here. I began to feel trapped by our circumstances, and I regretted my feelings of superiority over those miserable New Yorkers.

I needed some air. I went outside and walked through the dark around to the north side of my house, where the blueberry field runs up to the lawn. A major storm was blowing in—one of those epic collisions of Arctic and Atlantic fronts—and pounding gales charged across the meadow at thirty miles per hour, moaning against the gables of the house and stripping copper leaves off our giant oak. I gulped for air in the vacuum of the wind, and stiffened my knees to brace myself against the current, but it kept changing direction.

We woke Sunday to an October blizzard. Trees still bearing leaves sagged and snapped under white blankets as the wind whipped harder, and the snow fell faster.

12

If life is a series of lessons learned from mistakes, I should at this point rank highly as a dancer with the Bolshoi troupe. Yet although I have been stumbling across dance floors since before Baryshnikov defected, I am forever trying to keep up with graceful women as the band plays cruelly on. The first was my mother, herself a dance teacher; but for nearly two decades the feet I have most often stepped on belong to Sarah—who as a musician, singer, and former actress knows her way around a waltz, not to mention the mashed potato.

Actually it was an excess of mashed potatoes on Thanksgiving that led us to a contra dance the following night at the community center of St. Denis church in North Whitefield. A contra dance (the word is a variant of the French *contre danse*) is basically a line dance where partners face each other. But the choreography is endlessly mutable and dictated (literally) by a caller, who organizes the proceedings and makes sure that everybody dances with everybody else. The music can range from Cajun to old-time bluegrass and even Dixieland. Some friends who call themselves the Muddy Road String Band were playing at this dance. We needed some exercise. And Sarah's sister, a contra dance devotee, was goading us on. When we turned into the icy parking lot at nine, the band was already playing. We ducked in, tossed some bills into the untended cardboard cash box near the door, and peeled off our sweaters.

Despite its French name, St. Denis is a largely Irish congregation known for its community spirit. Unlike the coastal Catholic churches, which swell on summer Sundays, St. Denis serves a year-round rural community in central Maine. It's a twenty-four-seven operation, and on this frigid Friday night the joint was hoppin'.

Some of the older dancers were St. Denis parishioners, but not the dreadlocked student in Army fatigues and bare feet, or the deadhead couple doing those annoying wavy leg kicks. (Hey, even I could do that.) But they'd all be dancing with each other soon enough.

The musicians flashed smiles as we walked in: guitarist Toki Oshima, who is also an artist, and her husband John Pranio, who plays fiddle. The pianist and banjo man, John Gawler, hosts a bluegrass festival most summers at his farm on Buttermilk Hill. By day a sheet metal fabricator, he had restored the antique copper sink in our pantry. Behind him on the wall was a framed photo of John Paul II. Under the Pontiff were pictures of Maine monsignors, bishops, and nuns of note—most looking even sterner than Sister Madonna, the first-grade teacher who informed me within the space of two weeks that the president was killed and there was no Santa Claus.

The music surged as the dancers bowed and circled artfully. These were hardcore contra fans, and they acted as if everyone in America did this on Friday night. Sometimes life in rural Maine is so special that it feels like the Hollywood version of life in rural Maine. This would be the contra dance where Julia Roberts (who has fallen in love with a local farmer) do-si-dos with her beau's curmudgeonly father (who happens to be the first selectman, although Hollywood would call him the mayor) and screws up the dance in a wacky way that wins the hearts of all.

In real life, screwing up the dance just makes you feel dumb.

Contra dances should be great for leadfoots like myself because the caller barks out the moves over music. But in practice, it can get pretty confusing: "Okay men swing your neighbor's partner one and a half times now do-si-do across to the right now you're left of your partner take three steps in and stomp back and over again with a reverse out hands up and now down to the next . . ." My head was spinning, which I don't believe was one of the moves called for. This was an advanced dance, and we were out of our league.

When we reached the end of the line, we truly ran out of clues. Do we walk around to the front? Stand here like dopes? Dance with ourselves like Deadheads? Wait for the song to end? What should we do?

We defected.

If only we could step away from our farmhouse so easily. The past few weeks have found us torn with indecision over our home. None of the expensive renovations has made it any closer to the school, or the store. Sure, we could sell it—but selling old rural property takes months if not years to find the right buyer, and we'd be unlikely to get back our investment so soon after renovating. Yet we both know that there is no decision to make. This is the dance we paid for. Sometimes you get the chance to learn from your mistakes, but most often what you learn is how to live with them.

13

God is never far from the backcountry, which is nothing new, much less new age; my neighbors are simply religious, not spiritual. They don't connect, they worship. Toward the end of the year they worship more often, and not just because of Christmas. Every new winter brings a seasonal sadness to these parts, and religion helps in ways that folks just don't seem to need in summer when there's hay to cut and blueberries to rake until late at night.

And so it goes in our own life. Sarah recently found a small Episcopal church in Jefferson that she likes, so I came along one Sunday—curious but skeptical. I grew up Roman Catholic, which I consider to be more an ethnicity than a set of beliefs. Even though I rarely attend Mass and could never support the Church's ban on women priests, I still consider myself a Catholic and feel uncomfortable in churches with no weeping sculptures. Protestant services, like those stark Protestant churches, seem like stripped-down versions of the real thing to me. This Episcopal rite was closer to home, but I still couldn't help feeling it was Catholic Lite.

"I'm not sure I could support a church that basically exists because Henry the Eighth wanted to get divorced," I said on the drive home. "And that part where they call themselves Catholic; does the Pope know they're doing that?"

"It *is* Catholic," said Sarah. "It's just not Roman Catholic."

"Hey, whatever. Do they believe in the trans-substantiation?"

"Yes. But they don't have confession."

"That's outrageous."

"I thought you hated confession."

"Of course I hate confession; I'm Catholic, aren't I?"

It seemed clear that clarity would not come from the Church of England. It came, instead, about a week later, in a place I least expected: Allen Ginsburg's barn.

While working on a magazine story about midcoast Maine food purveyors, I found myself talking barns with Allen, co-owner of a Belfast granary called Fiddler's Green Farm. A former carpenter, Allen runs his grain mill in a modified post-and-beam barn that he built himself.

Building a barn was near the top of the priority list on our own farm. The original barn had long since burned, rotted or sagged into the earth; a few glacial foundation boulders were the only archeological reminders that a massive outbuilding once commanded the clearing behind the house. We had hoped to find a farm with a big old barn, but it wasn't so easy. There were plenty of romantic ruins, but we needed a barn that wasn't falling down. We want to raise sheep, store hay and tractors, maybe someday have horses. Bringing a sagging ruin back to life can cost more than building a new barn. So when we finally found what we thought was the right house, but no barn, we resigned ourselves to a major future building project.

"Major" is how several contractors described my ideal barn, with rough estimates coming in at around fifty thousand dollars. Lacking that much cash but desperate to build a big barn, I was hoping a veteran do-it-yourselfer like Allen could give me some advice on how to do it more cheaply.

"You don't happen to have a lot of tall pines on your property, do you?" he asked.

"I sure do," I said, thinking about my acreage across the road with its stand of white pines and hemlock.

"Then why don't you do what I did? Build your barn from your own trees. That's what everybody used to do, before they invented Georgia-Pacific. I know guys near you who can cut the trees, mill the wood, and yard it right on your land. It'll be rough-cut wood, but hey, it's a barn. They'll charge maybe twenty-five cents a board foot. You'll save thousands in lumber."

I saw immediately that it wasn't just about saving money. Here was an opportunity to say no thanks to the lumber companies, with their monoculture "forests" of perfect trees. Here was a chance to keep capital in my community by using local craftsmen and materials. With apologies to the hippie generation, here was a chance to grow my own.

Back home I pulled out my forest management plan and verified that as much as twenty-five thousand board feet of saw timber could be responsibly cut on that acreage—more than twice what I would need for a thirty-by-forty-foot barn. I was beginning to see my barn clearly for the first time. I could see myself lift the latch and heave open the creaking door. I imagined the smell of hay as the silent vastness engulfed me. I pictured the dusty ribbons of sunlight piercing the cracks in the siding, wrapping around rough-hewn beams and splitting the darkness into geometric voids.

A recent study found that seventy percent of Americans believe they can be spiritually "connected" without going to church, and I suppose I'm one of them. But the more I think about it, incense and hay don't smell too much different. Big barns are a lot like cathedrals, even if they don't have statues of saints in agony. Both put a roof over impossibly large spaces and make you feel small, but deeply connected to that which is larger. Would a barn built from my own woods groan in the wind like the tall pines are doing now?

Here was a religion I could call my own. But first I would have to do something even harder than going to confession. I would have to build my church.

14

SNOWPLOW PROCESSION PAYS HOMAGE
TO DRIVER

WINDSOR—Edwin Monroe, who had a passion
for plowing the snow from Maine's roads, was
doing what he loved to do most when he took ill
during a storm last week. A couple of hours after
the job was over, he was dead.

On Sunday, as yet another snowstorm threatened
a state already knee-deep in snow, a procession of a
dozen plow trucks followed Monroe's casket from
an old clapboard funeral home, over Maine's gray
and white winter landscape to a graveyard in this
central Maine farming town.
                    —Associated Press, February 5, 2001

L ife these days is so full of overpaid whiners that
when someone finds complete fulfillment behind a
snowplow, his funeral—just eight miles down the
road from me—makes the national news. Edwin Monroe,
the article goes on to report, plowed for fifty of his seventy-
nine years, having moved to Maine at age eighteen from
Connecticut, presumably seeking deeper snow.

It's been a busy year for the snowplow drivers in my corner of the state, although hardly a serious winter like they're having in the Midwest. I know; I grew up in Michigan and have been shoveling deep snow since I can remember. When I was eleven, I shoveled neighbors' driveways to earn money for the Beatles' *White Album*—which at roughly seven dollars was the most extravagant object I had craved in life up to that point. Recently when my own nine-year-old, a second-generation Beatles fan, asked if I would buy him the *White Album* ($24.48 on cdnow.com), I suggested he might shovel some snow. He stared at me blankly. Snow around our house is removed by a large motorized vehicle.

Snowplows are standard household equipment around here—none of those suburban snow "throwers," thank you. Just about every house has at least one plow hooked up to a Ford F-350 in the driveway, and usually a few more are lying around for parts or decoration. I have an ancient rusted snowplow sitting out in my blueberry field. It came with the house. I thought of getting rid of it, but it looks sort of like a Richard Serra sculpture, so I hang onto it.

I don't have a working snowplow, but some primeval Michigan gene compels me to clear my own driveway. So I invested in a sort of hybrid—a massive snow-throwing attachment for my John Deere lawn tractor.

This fifteen-hundred-dollar chunk of steel was an extravagance beyond my wildest dreams as a child saving money for a Beatles album, and I wish I could say it was worth it. Unfortunately, the chief problem is that lawn tractors are made to cruise lawns, not snow-covered driveways. They sit so low to the ground that even with chains and tire weights, they get stuck. And the engine, meant to turn a mower blade, doesn't rev high enough to move large amounts of wet white stuff. Meanwhile the tiny battery, again meant to crank over in August, often fails in February. It's easy to jumpstart with a car—assuming you can get a car through the new snow. If not, get out the shovel.

When the snow is average—say a few inches—I can quickly clear my driveway with its four-foot scoop. But in serious snowstorms like the recent drop, it goes more like this: engage thrower, release safety brake, shift to forward, move several inches—engine quits; shift to neutral, disengage thrower, apply safety brake, restart, release safety brake, engage thrower, reverse a foot, move forward a few more inches— engine quits; and so on. Three hours later, my short driveway was sort of cleared. When you consider that the late Edwin Monroe would have charged twenty dollars for doing the same job in a few minutes, it was a wasted morning.

Of course, just about everything I do around here would fail to impress an efficiency consultant. Raking and winnowing blueberries, pruning grape vines, pulling caterpillars off infested apple trees, and planting parsnips all cost much more in my time than they yield in produce. I do it for the lifestyle and to get outdoors—although rocking a conked-out lawn tractor through a raging blizzard was not part of the rural life I envisioned.

So I was ready to admit defeat when, later that day, a telemarketer called with a "special introductory offer to receive the *Portland Press Herald*."

"Save your breath," I said more or less politely. "No one will deliver here. We've tried."

"Sir," he said—in a vaguely sarcastic tone that suggested he really meant "You inbred country bumpkin"—"we wouldn't be calling you if the paper couldn't be delivered in your area."

"Oh yeah? That's what they said the last time. It never happens. But fine, I'll call your bluff. Sign me up."

The very next day he called me back. "Did you receive your paper?"

"Of course not. Where are you calling from?"

"Missouri."

"Well, up here we've got four feet of snow piled up along the roads. The street plow turned my mailbox into a tuna fish can, and even if we *had* a *Press Herald* box, it would be buried under a glacier at the end of my driveway. Say, do you get much snow down in Missouri?"

"Oh, some," he said loftily, as if trying to remember what snow looked like. I considered pitching him on a near-new John Deere snow thrower, but skipped it.

That would have been the end of the tractor fiasco were it not for my own hubris a week later, when I decided to clear out a walkway across my lawn. The lawn path had been my Waterloo several times, miring my tractor so badly that I had to tow it out with my truck. And Sarah was out of town, which made it even more stupid: I would have no one to help me. But the snow had melted down a bit, so off I went.

And I went a long way. Too far to reach with my truck. Then I got stuck. The wind was picking up and the temperature was dropping; I had to go to New York early the next morning. I knew if I didn't get it out right away, it would freeze in place, possibly until April. I kicked some snow and went for the shovel.

That's when I noticed the gaping holes in my greenhouse. Three large corrugated plastic roof panels were missing—gone with the wind. It appeared that although I had removed the heavy snowfall from the roof, the weight had bowed the panels enough to loosen them from their mounting brackets. All that remained were their trails through the snow—long straight gouges headed into my neighbor's hay field, a vast and windswept expanse of white. I set off through the snow and biting wind to find them, but soon found myself up to my crotch in impenetrable drifts.

I staggered back to the house and put on my snowshoes, but that was worse. With my first step the massive wooden shoes sank two feet into the drifts, pinning me in place as if caught in a bear trap. I had to dig with my hands through the snow and unstrap the shoes, yank them out and clomp back to the house.

My only hope was to set off down the road, hoping I'd catch sight of the panels blowing through the field. An hour later I had two of them in my house; the third was missing in action.

By then it was dark, and the mercury was sinking like a horseshoe. I didn't know it yet, but electricity was out all across the region; at least I still had lights. I gave up on the tractor and drove forty minutes to Belfast, where I was expected for dinner. I pulled into my aunt and uncle's driveway and beheld the Seventh Wonder of the World: a perfectly carved walkway through the snowdrifts, right to their welcome mat. "How did you do that?" I asked my uncle. "Just a regular two-stage snow thrower. Cost about seven hundred dollars. I cut paths all around the house."

"Does it ever get stuck?"

"Nah."

I came back from New York a few days later with the flu; Sarah's parents helped me heft the tractor out. Soon I'll have to deal with the greenhouse, but not until this fever breaks. I might even hire a local snowplow operator, someone who loves his job.

Three and a half years later I was foraging for mushrooms in my woods when I stumbled across the third greenhouse panel. It was in pretty good shape for all that time in the forest, so I dragged it into my cellar as a backup, having long since replaced it with a new one on the greenhouse. (I had also replaced my dysfunctional "snow tractor" with a sub-urban-style thrower like my uncle's; it works great.) Then, in May of 2004, a spring gale caught hold of another green-house panel, snapping it cleanly in half. Up came the old one from the cellar.

15

Geologists will tell you that mud has been around for a long time. Longer than dry ground, when you think about it. First came water, which covered the earth and gradually receded. Something had to happen between the primeval water and the primeval dry ground, and it would have been similar to what comes between winter and spring in Maine, except it lasted eons and nobody had rubber boots.

Mud doesn't get the respect that its age might command. Mud is ugly by any word. Mud is *slop, grime, slime, filth, muck, mire, sludge, slush, smut, ooze, glop, gunk, splosh, swill, smudge, grunge.* Even archaic words for mud are sloppy, like *slabby.* A repository for mud sounds even worse: it's a *muckhole,* a *bog* (which is the equally disgusting *gob* spelled backwards), a *quagmire,* a *sty,* a *hovel,* a *sump* or a *slough* (pronounced SLOO; the same word pronounced SLUF means the skin that a reptile sheds, or the verb that shakes it off). It's true that certain mudholes in the British Isles are called *loblollies,* which doesn't sound so bad unless your Vauxhall is stuck in one. But when a word that might mean mud sounds vaguely noble, like *midden,* it turns out to be a dung heap, which technically isn't mud at all. Mud rarely inspires, and in fact exists to disappoint.

Muddy verbs do not describe good deeds. Muddy thinking can *muddy* the waters, which is not the same as being Muddy Waters, who grew up on a plantation and knew the difference between midden and muck. Politicians *muck* things up—which is possibly worse than fucking things up, as they do when they *sling mud*. Putting snowmobiles and beer on credit cards gets Mainers *mired* in debt, but of course thrifty Yankees never get into that sort of *muddle*.

It's a muddy world out there, and defense demands constant vigilance. Thus we have *mudguards* on cars and *muckrakers* in journalism. An entire world war was fought in muddy trenches—a nasty quagmire that gave us the soldier's ironic toast *"Here's mud in your eye!"*

I parked in a muddy field at Rockland High School to attend the public supper for Ray Kelly. Ray is an English teacher at the school as well as my neighbor; his southwest alder bog ends at my northeast winterberry quagmire. Ray's wife Maddy is also a teacher, with Sarah at the Ashwood Waldorf School. Their daughter teaches at a public school in the Bronx. Last fall, Ray was diagnosed with ALS or Lou Gehrig's Disease, a degeneration of the motor neurons that has no cure. Some victims live for decades, but usually the disease results in total paralysis of the voluntary muscles, including those for speaking and swallowing, after three to five years.

Ray and Maddy are the kind of teachers who change kids' lives, so it wasn't surprising to see many of their devoted students among the more than eight hundred folks crowding into the gym for spaghetti and salad. The event raised more than four thousand dollars, some of which the school forced Ray to take; he wanted it all to go to the ALS Foundation.

In fact, Ray hasn't spent much time worrying about himself since his diagnosis. He is still teaching, even though symptoms of the disease are making it harder for him to make the forty-minute drive into Rockland every day. He is still serving as president of our Library Association, whose trustees manage the magnificent public library that was built in our tiny town in 1991—thirty years after the old library burned down along with the high school.

Last month, neighbors got together and figured out some practical ways to help Ray and Maddy. Helen, our resident massage therapist and healing expert, put together a list of chores to divvy up. Some people signed on to feed their farm animals; others will cook dinners. Sarah offered to help with housekeeping on weekends, and since I work at home I volunteered to drive Ray to doctor's appointments. Doctors are a long way from here, and I'm looking forward to spending some time with Ray in my truck.

I spoke to him briefly at the spaghetti supper, but it was difficult. The school's jazz band was running full-tilt through "In the Mood," which would have made it hard to converse even if Ray weren't having trouble speaking clearly. "That's so *nice* of you," he kept saying about our volunteer efforts. Because his speech is impaired, it's easy to assume he's muddled, but he's not. The disease does not affect intellect.

I had a hard time rounding up my nine-year-old after the supper; he was outside playing in the mud. Kids have no problem with mud. They are closer to the earth in every way, and they even have a word that makes mud sound okay: *mudpie.* I suppose children become adults when mud no longer feels good. But mud is just another season between life and death, and if you can learn anything about mud season from kids and Ray Kelly, it's that there is nothing to fear in the mire.

Ray Kelly died on January 31, 2002, at age 54.

16

One of the ways I differ from my neighbors is that I have an agent in New York. One of the ways I differ from my agent's other clients is that they are Hugely Famous Authors like John Berendt and Spalding Gray. I suppose that leaves me neither here nor there, yet in recent weeks I have spent a lot of time there—by which I mean on the phone with my agent, or leaving messages for my agent, or wondering why my agent hasn't called me back.

Like most writers, I have no taste for the practicalities of business; in my ideal workday I would write all morning, stroll out to the mailbox and collect the day's checks and literary accolades (dropping the utility bills on Sarah's desk), followed by lunch and a nap. But because I am in the process of selling a book about building my own barn, I must care, at least temporarily, about advances and art budgets and foreign rights.

My agent is ideally suited to handle these matters. She is smart and she speaks in that worldly, abbreviated New York way that makes you sit up straight and pay attention. You want an agent who encourages good posture while taking a percentage of your money. When we do chance to find each other on the phone, our conversations go like this:

SHE: Random House likes the idea but they're troubled by the fact that the barn isn't built yet.

ME: So am I.

SHE: It's not about the writing. They love the writing—other than saying give us Marcel Proust, which is what they always say.

ME: Well, we could call the book *Remembrance of Barns Past.*

And so on. But then she called me on a Saturday, which was odd. "Here's what's happening," she said in an excited voice that sent my mind racing. How many millions did she get for the book, I wondered? Will Tom Hanks play me in the movie?

"I've just taken the job as co-head of the literary department at the William Morris Agency."

"Wow," I replied. "That's great news." It even made the *New York Times* on Monday. It also turned out to be news that would cost me money, as her new agency charges authors fifteen percent, versus ten percent at the old agency—but as I said, business details leave me cold. At any rate, I figured it would take her several weeks to learn the new secret handshake, so I forgot about my book and turned my attention to weightier matters: it was time for my town's annual local election and meeting. Decisions made at this level would definitely not make the *New York Times*, but they would affect my life much more directly than anything happening in midtown Manhattan.

The first item on the ballot was the election of our version of a mayor, who goes by the title of First Selectman, Assessor and Overseer of the Poor. I voted for the incumbent, Wesley, who has proven to be one of the more conservation-minded town elders. That's important because basically, my town is divided into two parts: Those who want more gravel pits, and those who don't.

One wants to sympathize with landowners who can make far more money strip-mining gravel than growing cabbage. These are people who have lived off this land, their family's land, for generations—farming, logging, wreath-making, they've tried it all. They don't have an agent in New York.

And yet one cannot imagine these pastoral ridges stripped of topsoil and riven by gravel pits, nor support developments that destroy centuries-old rural landscapes for short-term gain.

But the annual town meeting, which is always held the day after the election, is generally a decorous affair despite the bubbling resentments. Rarely will someone fire a broadside like "How can we keep these city people from moving into our town?" It's more of a social event, and this year some seventy-five townsfolk showed up to munch on cookies baked by the ladies of the Evening Star Grange, pick up a free smoke detector from the volunteer fire department, and congratulate Wesley, who beat his opponent by a margin of seventy-four votes—a relative landslide in a turnout of just four hundred forty-four voters.

Much closer was the vote to ban jet-skis on the local pond, which squeaked over the line with just seven votes. But a new mining ordinance to tighten restrictions on gravel pits failed—by nineteen votes.

Most of the meeting was devoted to public approval of dozens of minute budget items—everything from graveyard flags (three hundred dollars) to street-light maintenance (two thousand two hundred dollars). You might think such mundane matters would pass without comment; not in my town. Someone stood up and demanded to know why we have to pay two thousand five hundred dollars for firefighter physicals. (It's required by state law, replied Tom the fire chief.) Someone else wondered why the town was giving one thousand one hundred eighty-five dollars to the Red Cross and only eight hundred dollars to the town's own Food Bank; shouldn't we have allotted more to the local charity? (The Red Cross requests a donation of one dollar per resident, someone replied—and at any rate the international relief organization does help locally, especially after house fires.)

And so on. The meeting wore on, and when it ended I was tired. I drove home past the gravel pits, checked my mailbox, and took a nap. I woke up to a much bigger controversy than Red Cross donations. The mother of all zoning battles had just landed right in our town. It might as well have been *War of the Worlds*.

I Hear America Singeing

(The Third Year)

17

If you should ever wake up on a fine spring morning and discover that the eighth largest road-building company in America thinks your little town would be an excellent place for a fifty-six-acre granite quarry with a rock crushing operation and two manufacturing plants—one for concrete and one for asphalt—here is what you must do:

First, you must listen carefully to the phoebes, vireos, and grosbeaks in your oak tree. They won't tell you what to do, but you may never hear them again.

Then you must form a non-profit opposition group, and join it.

I am not a joiner by inclination, typically finding a way to distance myself even from causes that merit participation. I dropped out of the Maine Organic Farmers and Gardeners Association after learning they forbid coffee at their annual fair (oh, please). I'm not antisocial but I count only a few close friends, most of whom go back with me for decades. I'm perfectly happy working alone at home for days on end. I don't say any of this with pride; I strive to open more doors in my life—and opportunity just came knocking.

Here then is the backstage view of Maine's development woes: As coastal communities in the southern half of the state cope with suburban sprawl and Wal-Mart contagion, rural towns like mine are being raped for the raw materials to pave that sprawl. As Robert Kennedy Jr. points out in his book *The Riverkeepers*, poor communities are often victimized by a form of environmental redlining: heavily polluting industries establish beachheads in such areas, where citizens have limited power of protest. The industry may well provide jobs but it also makes the community less desirable as a place to live; people who can afford to leave (generally those who pay the most taxes) move away, initiating a downward spiral that undermines the tax base and ultimately transforms the town into an industrial zone. Environmental redlining is not a problem in affluent communities, because property is too valuable for industry. But of course, the property is valuable precisely because there is no industry. It works out pretty well for the rich.

When the dust settles—and strip mines make plenty of dust—it's all about gravel, a primary component of roadbuilding. But this is not just another gravel pit. That's because natural gravel, like fossil fuel, seems to be running out. At any rate, it's not uniform enough for today's more stringent engineering standards. The solution now is to blast schists of granite ledge out of the earth, then mechanically crush it into perfectly sized gravel-like aggregate. Add limestone and sand, and you have concrete; add petroleum and you get asphalt.

Add one hundred trucks per hour on town roads where children wait for school buses. Add the Damariscotta Lake watershed, in which the site is located. Add the town's major aquifer, under or adjacent to the blasting zone. Add plummeting real estate values, which in fact are impossible to add because no one has been able to sell a house here since the proposal was announced. Add a zoning ordinance that prohibits manufacturing in the district. Add a town planning board with open contempt for the zoning ordinance they are charged to enforce.

Add the Lane Construction Corporation of Connecticut, which earns three hundred fifty million dollars a year—more than enough to lease fifty-six acres of granite from a farmer who needs money and is an easy target for exploitation.

Add torches and pitchforks on a starry night humming with blackflies, and you get a public hearing in my town in May.

At the hearing you must demand that the planning board, whose chairman is a used-car dealer, retain qualified experts to evaluate the complex proposal. You'll want to print up lawn signs that say "Lane, Lane, Go Away!" and put them all around town.

If you're lucky, you'll have a lawyer like Bo, who happens to live next door to the quarry site. Bo put his own practice on hold to secure a paper trail for the inevitable court challenges. The fight has exhausted but inspired him; when the dust settles, he may even decide to specialize in zoning law.

You may find in your town a bearded, old-school activist like Dave, who specializes in irony and also happens to be president of the North American Vexillological Association. Vexillology is the study of flags, which can come in handy; Dave once protested that an annual town meeting could not legally come to order without the presence of an American flag. He went on to observe that the solid green curtain draping the stage was in fact the flag of Libya, and did the town want to hold its annual meeting under the standard of Muammar al-Qaddafi? An American flag was quickly procured.

You might have a citizen like Vic, a polar bear of a man and a former U.S. Marshal from New York City. Vic is our unofficial investigator, spending hours quizzing citizens in other towns where Lane has operations, as well as poring over court and municipal records from Augusta to Belfast. Vic is the sort of fellow who knocks you over with a friendly backslap. He introduces himself at public meetings as "Bigmouth," except in his New-Yorkese it comes out "Bigmout."

Or you could turn to someone like Sandy, who raises Arabian horses just over the hill from the Lane site. Sandy is a gentle force who knocks on doors, gathers signatures and gets timid neighbors to speak up. She would make a good selectman, if not a governor.

Soon you might notice a new spirit in your town, and in yourself. At that point you might step back and appreciate the higher wisdom that is behind even adversity like strip mines. If Lane was banking on bumpkins, they were in for a surprise.

So was I. Until now I had no idea that my little town was home to so many people who, like us, had fled the Rest of America, and for similar reasons. And I met old-timers who were also shocked at the prospect of an asphalt plant, although most were reluctant to speak up. But we were many and we had come far to this place, whether by ancestry or by design, and we were not ready to be redlined.

18

The first car to hit the skunk must have been small—not anything like a fully loaded gravel truck, the primary form of vehicular transport along my country road. When *Mephitis mephitis* meets bituminous hot-top under the double-wheel of a dump truck, the evidence is pretty much destroyed. But this skunk was still a fully formed specimen, ready for the taxidermist. There he was, with V-shaped white markings identifying him clearly as the common striped skunk.

Skunks are members of the weasel family and are said to be quite tasty. Maine's Penobscot Indians used to eat them regularly. They were careful to remove the scent gland (located within the anus), and not just because it smells so noxious. The offending chemical, a sulfuric compound called butylmercaptan, is in fact a nerve poison that can be fatal if ingested. An angry skunk can squirt the stuff sixteen feet, but with pinpoint accuracy only up to nine feet. Either way, the stink travels as far as a half mile.

That's under laboratory conditions. Factor in a hot summer on a back road in Maine, with multiple tire encounters, and I believe you can double that distance. Every day for two weeks that skunk got flatter and flatter, and smellier and smellier, until finally he was découpaged into the pavement and the whole town could pick up the scent.

Dead skunks are supposed to get picked up long before they turn into folk art. But backcountry towns like mine are broke in summer; last winter's snowplowing bill has just been paid off, and the new tax bills don't get mailed out until August. High summer is when small Maine towns cut way back—which is in stark contrast to the citizens, who, reeling in cash from the summer people, are ready to tap a few kegs.

It makes for a strange tension around town, between ornery selectmen trying to pay the warrants and devil-may-care residents bent on a good time—especially when your town is trying to fend off a proposed asphalt plant that would spew fifty-five tons of sulfuric compounds into our air every year. That's more sulfur than several million skunks emit, but the plant would mean more dead skunks too, once its trucks start rumbling down our roads.

Concern about the Lane Construction plant heated up last week when the town's lawyer submitted a two thousand seven hundred dollar bill for his work on the hearings over the last two months. Our land use ordinance allows us to charge legal expenses to the applicant—a reasonable notion given that the plant is, after all, their idea. But some of our town officials can't see burdening a huge Connecticut corporation with legal bills that might have been avoided if a bunch of uppity citizens hadn't decided to protest the plant in the first place. If the taxpayers want to get all persnickety about a little sulfur dioxide pollution, let them pay the legal bill.

Jim, a local accountant and former state legislator who's also on the town budget committee, gave a report to the planning board chairman that ended with stark reasoning: "It's like this, Bradley. The town has no money. If we don't get Lane to pay the lawyer, we can't have a lawyer any more."

Taking a lead from Shakespeare, someone suggested that not having a lawyer might be a good thing. But given that the neighborly folks from Lane have two lawyers at every hearing, it was decided after much chin-rubbing that the town should probably have at least one.

Lane was ordered to pay, but some officials still grumbled about how a bunch of whining citizens were driving the town to financial ruin. Some even hinted darkly that the biggest complainers were "folks from away," although the accusers did not offer to eat skunk as a demonstration of their own native heritage. At any rate, the storm passed quickly because the summer people are up, the ice cream stand is crowded, and the locals are making money. Besides, it was time for the big summer opening at the Downtown Art Gallery.

The two things in my town of thirteen hundred that strangers are always surprised to see are its beautiful public library (staffed entirely by volunteers) and its very of-the-moment art gallery—actually a cooperative run by several local artists. Perhaps because it's off the coastal tourist beat, the Downtown Gallery doesn't traffic in lighthouse paintings; it puts on sophisticated exhibits by serious Maine artists. Its openings are festive affairs that draw a curious mix of locals in work boots and Soho refugees in black Nehru shirts and brocade vests. Last week we all came down to check out new landscapes by Lorna Crichton and Joan Freiman while sipping wine and engaging in our own novel brand of small-town summer chatter: comparing asphalt plant emission studies, and reminding each other to remove our "Lane, Lane Go Away!" road signs so the shoulder mower can get through.

"If he has to stop and move the signs, it'll cost the town money," someone warned. You see, it's July, and the town is broke.

Sarah and I went out to round up our kids, who were climbing on the town's war memorial. Many of the names engraved in that cold stone are families that still work the land here, reminding us that freedom comes at a particularly heavy price for small towns. I decided we should thank God when the bill for democracy comes from the lawyer—as opposed to the stonecutter and the undertaker.

19

I mogene Coca just died at age ninety-two, and I wasn't surprised when *TV Guide* called with the assignment to write a tribute. Because I generally refuse to watch television, I get what *TV Guide* calls the "nostalgia" stories that don't require an encyclopedic knowledge of the characters on *Friends*.

This would be easy. The format called for some touching remembrances and humorous anecdotes from those who knew Coca, who was the wacky partner of Sid Caesar in the classic 1950s TV revue *Your Show of Shows*. I'd interviewed the key people from *Your Show of Shows*—Carl Reiner, Mel Brooks, Neil Simon, and Caesar himself, among others—several times over the years. A few quick calls to some Hollywood bigmouths and I'd be out on Dyer Long Pond, reeling in the smallmouths, before dinner.

Alas, the bass got a break. Comedian Brooks had just won eight million Tony Awards for the Broadway version of his 1968 film *The Producers*, and his surly office lady snapped that he was "not doing any press that wasn't about the Tonys." This was frustrating because I knew that once I got Mel on the phone, he would never stop talking.

On to Neil Simon, whose assistant promptly requested The Dreaded Fax. Hollywood is the last holdout on Earth for the fax machine. Everybody else on the planet uses e-mail, but in Hollywood the only way to interview a Major Person is by sending a groveling fax on magazine letterhead, outlining the nature of the interview request. When I was an editor at *People* we had a strict policy against faxing interview requests—on the grounds that it was inappropriately hat-in-hand, and at any rate what about *People* did the publicist not understand? Was she unfamiliar with the magazine? We actually lost some stories that way, with interview requests devolving into playground spats:

"You *must* send a fax."

"No, I *won't* send a fax."

"But you *must* send a fax."

"Well, I *won't* send a fax."

"Then you can't talk to Mr. Bigshot."

"Then Mr. Bigshot can't be in our magazine. So there."

It was embarrassing. But most magazines accede to the fax request, so there I was faxing at my desk instead of casting on the pond.

Carl Reiner's people said the star was on vacation and not taking any interview requests. I sighed; Reiner is a clever guy who always told me great stories. When he says "Here's a good one," you push the Record button. I knew he would want to talk, but I could tell his office staff was just afraid to bother him. What they didn't know was that I had his home phone. So I rang him up directly and left an urgent message.

Caesar himself was easy to reach. But he's a nonverbal sort to begin with, and lately he's been ailing; tired and hard of hearing, the TV legend had little to say about Coca beyond how much he loved her. I asked him to explain their chemistry and he replied: "You don't look a gift horse in the mouth."

I rang Howard Morris, a forgotten co-star on *Your Show of Shows* and a close friend of Coca's. He picked up the phone at his house and said that Coca's battle with Alzheimer's had left her unable to recognize him in recent years. When I replied that Caesar told me the same thing, Morris said, "Yeah, well, you have to *like* somebody to recognize them." This was getting ugly.

Other events were conspiring to keep me off the pond. While strolling through my meadow, I noticed some black gunk oozing up from the ground. It was crude but definitely not oil. The septic analyst from Windsor came over the next day and said "Ah-yuh, you need a new septic system. That'll be seventy-five dollars."

"What do I do now?"

"Get Dave Studer to design you a septic system," he said, handing me the bill. "Once he draws up a plan, fax it over to me." (Score one for the fax!)

A true flatlander, my neighbor Dave Studer was born in North Dakota and raised in Kansas. His father's dream of becoming a scientist was dashed by color-blindness that hampered his ability to observe natural phenomena. So he became a minister instead—color-blindness being an asset in that field—and Dave grew up the son of a preacher man. Dave inherited his dad's love of science and after college found himself teaching the subject in a Washington, D.C. public school, to seventh- and eighth-graders who had been thrown out of other schools. "The first thing you need to know," said the principal on Dave's first day, "is don't bother calling their parents." Many of his students were already parents themselves.

Dave went on to get a Master's degree in environmental education, and now he applies his knowledge of soil structure to the design of septic systems. But the professor in him loves to expound—and like Mel Brooks, once you get him going there's no end in sight. Dave could go on for hours about what goes down the toilet, and the science of sinkers and floaters—which, come to think of it, so could Mel Brooks. Dave came over and we dug holes in my field and sat in the tall grass and sifted dirt between our fingers while he showed me where centuries of plowing gave way to compacted subsoil, and how oxygen reached into my ground and turned the iron bright orange, and where the seasonal water table peaked, and how to hear the sand in your land by rubbing a clump next to your ear.

Carl Reiner called me back with a neat anecdote about the time Edward R. Murrow got Imogene Coca tipsy before a TV interview. Thanks, Carl. May your subsoil always drain deep.

20

The truth is, I hadn't planned to repair my sagging sheep shed on John Henry Day. I didn't even know our country had a special day in honor of the mythical freed slave who used two twenty-pound hammers to carve West Virginia's Big Bend railroad tunnel faster than a steam drill. But when I heard on the radio that morning about John Henry Day, I felt it was a good sign.

I felt I needed John Henry. The sheep shed that came with the deed to my land is beyond primitive; indeed to call it a structure would be to use the word in vain. Archeological evidence suggests that it was once a 16-by-18-foot gable-roofed enclosure, open on two sides, eight feet high at the peak and supported by eight massive hemlock trunks set about two feet into the earth. Running on top of those trunks are hand-hewn oak barn beams recycled from a much earlier (and better made) building, each one weighing more than a large asteroid. The rafters are simply pine logs, stripped of bark and crudely shaped with a hatchet. They in turn support a roof of rough-cut inch-thick pine boards so rotten that a pocket knife cuts through them like Styrofoam. Both roof and siding have so many jagged cracks that sunlight streams through in crazed patterns—resembling one of those modern churches with Expressionistic stained-glass windows.

After decades of neglect, the carpenter ants and nor'easters had eaten and beaten my shed down, down, down—forty-five degrees down, more or less, to the point where it was downright dangerous. I would have to pull it up with a two-ton hand winch called a come-along, then replace the rotten hemlock trunks with pressure-treated six-by-six posts set in concrete, then replace the rotten roof.

Fortunately I had solicited the help of my father-in-law, but like myself he is a writer, and thus of the head-scratching school of carpentry. We managed to get the come-along rigged up between a large white pine and the shed, and we even managed to start pulling the building straight. But it groaned and creaked, and the ancient beams wobbled dangerously. It was scary and unpredictable, and we were wondering what to do next when John Henry arrived.

"My name eez Pierre," he said, extending a hand. Pierre, it turns out, was the husband of a former graduate-school classmate of Sarah's; they had come up from Kennebunk for the day, and he had wandered out back to see what all the fuss was about.

In the pantheon of French musclemen, Pierre was no André the Giant. He was in fact a man of average height and weight, but he had the deep tan and rippled biceps of someone who works hard, and outdoors. I explained our project as sweat tumbled down my brow, and asked if he had any bright ideas. "Well, perhaps we take a look," he said. "I am a *carpentaire*."

Out of misplaced respect for our own efforts, Pierre le Carpentaire was at first diplomatic in his advice. "Eef I may say some-zing about your lev-*elle*," he began daintily. "A two-foot lev-*elle* on zees span is really inadequate. Much bettaire you use ze eye-*ball*."

We looked eyeball to eyeball and decided to use Pierre's eyeball—and any other body parts he could spare. In a flash he was hefting beams, planting posts, sawing boards, and driving spikes with a sledgehammer. Had the shed required cleaning, I am certain he could have diverted a river through it. He explained how its original builder failed to properly brace the structure, and showed me how to do it right.

When it came time to notch out a crossbeam, Pierre suggested we use a circular saw to dig out a channel, then chisel out the remaining wood. I was familiar with that technique but pointed out that the shed was too far to reach with my hundred-foot extension cord. "No problem," he said, pointing to my Stihl, "we use ze chainsaw."

Chainsaw carpentry is, of course, a distinctly Maine-based branch of the applied arts, so I was curious to see how a Frenchman would rise to this native woodworking task. Minutes later he stood in a pile of sawdust as we admired the near-perfect joint he had fashioned with a tool meant for demolishing trees.

It turns out Pierre was from a region of France that is at least spiritually akin to Maine—the rugged and remote central department called the Auvergne. The Auvergnat are no-nonsense woodsy types who shake their heads disapprovingly at the air-kissing sophisticates of Paris. As it happens, I have spent a fair amount of time in the Auvergne, and Pierre and I talked wistfully of cabbage soup and goose stew.

When it came time for lunch we hauled out a leftover roast chicken, and green beans from our garden; Pierre's wife Marta produced a loaf of bread from their car, as well as a round of blue cheese from the Auvergne that they apparently never travel without. I asked Pierre what he wanted to drink, but I already knew the answer. We washed it all down with a jug of red wine.

21

John Waters didn't bother saying hello. He just got on the phone and started yelling. I needed a quote from the director about the '50s movie hunk Troy Donahue, who had just died. I was writing his obit for *TV Guide*, and Waters had directed Donahue in the 1990 teen-pic send-up *Cry-Baby*. I quickly learned that the filmmaker had a "history" with the magazine, which meant he hated it, which meant I had to listen to his tirade before we could get to the sound-bite. "Every time I do your magazine, they don't print it or they edit it and change what I say!" he shouted. "I've had very bad experiences. This is my last shot with them; if they do it again I'm never talking to them. If they want answers that are normal, they shouldn't call me!"

He had a point. Waters is certainly not "normal" by most standards. But when you live in rural Maine, a guy who makes movies watched by millions of Americans seems, in a perverse way, pretty normal. Compare that to people whose only form of winter heat is chopping down trees on their own land. Or guys who carry tampons in their jacket pockets to stop the bleeding from chainsaw cuts when they're deep in the woods. People in my town don't live anything close to normal American twenty-first-century lives. The nearest place to see a John Waters movie is twenty-five miles away. In today's America, that's not normal.

Which helps explain why folks in my neck of the woods are having a hard time with President Bush's call for *patriotic spending* to teach those terrorists a thing or two about consumer confidence. Never mind his bizarre exhortation that we all pack up the kids, right now, this week, and fly to Disney World. (Doesn't he know school is back in session? Isn't he "the education president?") To rural Mainers, it seems downright un-American to spend money on anything. When folks in my town heard that a teaspoonful of anthrax could wipe out the whole state, they appreciated the frugality.

So when locals needed to stock up on American flags, they didn't drive to Wal-Mart in Rockland, thirty miles away, and fill their carts with made-in-China flags. They just trotted over to Dave's house. Being president of the North American Vexillological Society, Dave has lots of flags lying around. He mainly works as a computer consultant to small businesses, but he is also a professional appraiser of antique flags through his website, www.vexman.net.

When I dropped by Dave's farmhouse last week, he was sold out of current American flags and making plans to travel to Philadelphia for an appearance on the History Channel. He'd already done about twenty-five interviews since the terrorist attacks. The tall flagpole in his front yard was flying two huge banners: a thirteen-starred American flag and the so-called Gadsden flag—the famous 1776 image of a snake with the motto "Don't Tread On Me."

You wouldn't want to tread on Dave—a stout, bearded,

Jerry Garcia type who laughs easily but also gets worked up over Things That Matter. He took the reins of the North American Vexillological Society in 1998, after a controversy over inclusion. "Basically some of the group's leaders felt that *North America* meant white guys in the U.S. and Canada," he says. "I didn't agree with that, so I got involved."

A New Jersey native, Dave got hooked on flags as a freshman in high school, when he wrote a report on the flag of Wales (white and green with a dragon) for English class. "There's an old saying that flags are the shorthand of history," he says. "You can often tell the whole story of a country in its flag."

Dave arrived in Maine from Boston, where he had driven a taxi. "One night a guy put a gun upside my head and said 'Leave the money, get out, start walking and don't look back,'" says Dave. "So I did what he said. Then the cab company sued me for loss of their vehicle. I fought them for two years. When we finally got in front of a judge, he said 'Are you kidding?' and threw out their suit. By then I'd had my apartment ripped off twice and two cars stolen."

It was 1974. He moved to Maine, and didn't look back.

The current flag mania is unprecedented in American history—no such run on Old Glory followed Pearl Harbor or any other national tragedy—and Dave attributes it to the nature of the devastation. "These were attacks on powerful American symbols," he says, "so we turn to a symbol in response."

Dave has no plans to visit Disney World, and from the looks of his well-used kitchen woodstove, his spending patterns are not likely to boost many stocks on the Big Board. Sorry, Mr. Bush. Dave's as patriotic as any American—a flag-waving radical with a deep respect for history, and the wisdom to be happy with what he has. If you want normal, flag down someone else.

22

ITEN IN A MAIL-ORDER CATALOG:

A. Folding Writing Desk **EXCLUSIVE**
Sturdy, foldable, portable, and a bargain. The perfect desk for a small space or sudden urge to write . . . *No rush or express delivery.*

B ack, fickle muse!—my desk is in the mail! In real life, my sudden urges to write are inspired by calendar notes like *SEWAGE TREATMENT STORY DEADLINE TODAY!!!* Until then, I'm out clearing land, liming fields, and stacking firewood.

Which got me thinking: Am I blue collar or white collar? And when do I have to decide? "You're definitely white collar," said Sarah over dinner the other night. "You earn a living at a computer." But a few minutes later she stared at me and said, "Oh my God, your eyebrow hairs are so long, they're curling back into your skull!"

"See, I *am* blue collar."

Well, maybe. But as any self-respecting self-help guru will tell you, life is all about balance. It goes something like this: a pound of fresh, wet cow manure is equivalent to a page of writing. Shovel some, write some. When you reduce problems to their essence—and there's plenty of essence around here—the clouds part.

So here is a typical, if theoretical, week ripped from the headlines, as they say, of my desk calendar:

MONDAY:

1. Write article for do-it-yourself magazine about home security systems; play up terrorism angle, per editor.

2. County extension officer comes at 10:00 to discuss pasture management.

TUESDAY:

Mulch fruit trees, re-caulk greenhouse.

Revise proposal for how-to book on moving to Canada.

WEDNESDAY:

Write article for home magazine on adding a library wing; include info on where to buy fake book spines to hide big screen TV. (Note editor's advice: "Our readers aren't do-it-yourselfers, they're *buy*-it-yourselfers.")

Town Mining Standards Committee Meeting: Vote on controversial proposal to ban gravel pits from elementary school playground.

THURSDAY:

Come up with theme for Woodstock-type music

festival in my blueberry field. (Rejected ideas: Free drugs—too expensive; naked dancing—too cold; camping in the mud—too dry; benefit post-9/11 New York—New Yorkers might come.)

Re-work book proposal on ethnic restaurants to reflect stay-at-home comfort theme, per agent in New York. ("We need to get *prairie* in the title, but don't make it seem forced.")

FRIDAY:

Buck and split maple limbs left by Central Maine Power trimmers on side of my road; chase turkeys out of winter rye patch.

Contact Etta James management to inquire on availability (with full Muscle Shoals horn section) to headline concert in my field (theme: Fight the Zeitgeist!); petition selectmen to allow 50,000 concertgoers to park along town roads; check on need for portable toilets (DEP: Are trees a viable alternative?).

Trim eyebrow hairs.

It feels good to have that balance. One of the ugly truths about September 11 is that before the attacks, many office workers regularly fantasized about their buildings disappearing. There is something oppressive about vast, monolithic places of work. I know; I spent years in such buildings, in both lower and midtown Manhattan as well as on Wilshire Boulevard in Los Angeles. The way we feel about our workplaces is unhealthy, and not just because skyscrapers have become scary targets. Work is now an out-of-body experience for most Americans; it's something you do way over there, in that specialized building with its T-1 computer lines, recycled air, and "health clubs" (a cruelly vicarious way of getting exercise without getting a stack of wood). Office buildings don't even have proper street addresses anymore. Where exactly was "One World Trade Center Plaza," anyway? Just try that with your house.

I know we can't go back to the pre-industrial era, when everyone worked at home. But if we are to be a nation of corporate Bartlebys and buy-it-yourselfers, some adjustments are in order. While we're trying to understand the Middle East from our TV screens and computer terminals, let's also think about how we can use technology so more people can perform their scrivening closer to their homes, and make work a part of their real life. Otherwise we risk a future controlled by the gizmos (including high-tech skyscrapers) that we invent—rather like that presented in the film *2001*.

Technology is great, but sometimes manure is better. For me, a good day involves some downloading—and some truck loading. At the exact moment terrorists struck, I was up on the peak of my sheep shed, trimming the edge of some rolled roofing. It was hard work and I cursed as the craft knife slipped and wobbled through the thick asphalt, but it was the last step of a building project I had spent much of the summer on, beginning with that fortuitous day when Pierre showed up. Afterwards, I stood back and admired my amateur but capable work; it looked better than the roof a pro had put on my henhouse last summer, and I did it myself. An hour later, checking my e-mail, the day turned immeasurably bad.

I'm happy I don't work in Manhattan any more, even if my "tech support" now consists of a paperclip to restart my computer. But when my Mac crashes on deadline, I never get the urge to throw it out the window. I go outside and toss around some manure.

23

The holiday season in rural Maine during wartime looks a lot like the holidays during peacetime, but with more flags. This presents a problem around the average Maine farmhouse because in a typical Christmas season the styrene Santas, chipboard reindeer, glow-in-the-dark snowmen, icicle lights, and foam candy canes need only compete for space with the leftover orange jack-o-lantern leaf bags and aerosol cobwebs. Adding Old Glory to the decorative mix is a bit like gilding the gild on the (plasticene) lily.

But the question of how to simultaneously deck the halls and wave the flag is not exactly an aesthetic challenge around here, where the notion of economy applies to car parts, not lawn ornaments. There is a good deal of suspicion in this region about the Modernist tenet that *less is more*, which sounds like double talk invented by flatlanders who read magazines and, worse, want to save trees. If less were more, why don't they sell *small* eggs? In fact the problem around here boils down to a riddle of physics, the square footage available for decoration on any farmhouse exterior being finite.

I was pondering this local philosophy of *more is more* on the way to Thanksgiving dinner at Sarah's parents. Although her grandfather is still alive and relatively healthy at age 91, Sarah's father Bob and stepmother Annabelle have become the de facto patriarch and matriarch of the clan, in part because all their offspring live near them in Maine. Here then was truly a celebration of more—sixteen people around one impossibly medieval board. Squeezing everyone in was like watching the entire Basie band perform in one of those Greenwich Village nightclubs, where the trombone player needs permission from air traffic control to hit a low note. "If you need to use the bathroom you'd better go before you sit down," said Annabelle, and she wasn't kidding—once in place you were pinned, and all you could pass was the gravy.

Besides, as they say in the ads for horror movies, no one would hear you if you screamed. Sarah's family is not the brooding, melancholic type, or even the repressed, WASP-y type. Everyone pretty much has something to say, and it's often about fishing.

Thanksgiving is a good time to talk about fishing because you can't actually fish, November falling as it does between the end of the open-water season and the start of ice fishing. So Sarah started talking about the first time her dad took her fishing. It was around her ninth birthday in the summer of '67, and they went to the hardware store and picked out a spiffy junior rod and push-button casting rig. At the fishing hole, which was actually a high bridge over a slow-moving stream, Bob gave her careful instructions and a casting demonstration. Sarah pushed the button, cocked back her new rod and sent the line flailing out over the abyss.

"Let go! Let go!" cried her dad. Of course, he meant let

go of the button. But Sarah, who has always been a good listener, heard exactly what he said. Less, in this case, was not more.

She let go of the rod.

Her father doesn't remember much about that day; the image of a brand-new rod and reel cartwheeling into the drink had been repressed. "What did I do then?" he asked.

"I think you were pretty angry but you managed to control it," she recalled. "You said something like 'Well, that's all the fishing for today.'"

Nobody in Sarah's family cares much about football, and at any rate, her parents don't own a TV, so Thanksgiving entertainment is bring-your-own-banjo. Bob and his brother Laird are both banjo pickers, and both have played professionally on and off for decades. But it's mostly out of passion; you get the feeling they love old-time music way too much to turn it into a mere living. They've been playing and listening together since they were kids, and they collect obscure 19th-century instruments and they know that the 1948 "MTA Song" ("He may ride forever 'neath the streets of Boston . . . ") is just a remake of the traditional "Wreck of Old '97," and they can sing either one from memory. It's not the kind of thing you learn by watching TV.

Once they start playing, it's hard to tell them apart. One will start a song, strumming out a few chords and the first verse, then the other picks up and joins in on the chorus, and soon their neck muscles are stretched tighter than kite strings and their hands are flying up and down the frets and they're both wailing out the words until one or the other takes a solo and starts popping strings and bobbing his head, and pretty soon it's just a blur of beards and banjos.

Two bearded brothers on banjo can make a lot of noise, but they need more. They need a third brother on guitar. The third brother, Stuart, was young and strong, except in one tiny, fatal way, and now he is gone and Sarah plays the guitar. Nobody talks much about Stuart because it's still too hard, but his memory hangs over every song like a Christmas tree ornament that's a little too heavy for its branch. Every now and then one of the two brothers will mention The Reunion, which was the last time the three brothers played together.

The Reunion was a 1996 family gathering at a camp in Virginia's Blue Ridge Mountains, and in Sarah's family it has become the fulcrum of Before and After. "There's a dark and a troubled side of life," sings one brother as he strikes up the 1906 gospel classic. "There's a bright, there's a sunny side, too. . . . "

But there's more. There's Sylvia, who is Stuart's widow, one of the most delightful people I have ever known—which made her utter devastation at his loss all the more painful to observe. Yet there she was at the Thanksgiving table, laughing, possibly louder than a banjo.

24

An optical principle of rural Maine truer than Brunelleschi's law of perspective states that on even the most rundown farm, a camera can be so positioned as to avoid the mountain of cow dung, the used tire dump, the snowmobile graveyard, and the neighboring gravel pit. A skilled photographer at that vantage point can, with the use of a telephoto lens smeared liberally with petroleum jelly, compose a shot encompassing the one remaining side of the house where paint hasn't peeled, the one remaining goat since the coyotes breached the fence, and the one remaining hand of the happily waving back-to-the-lander, who learned about hydraulic tractor hitches the hard way.

This is the shot that appears in the trendy home magazine, above a caption which reads: "'Running this farm is hard work,' says John (with a basket of organic mizuna ready for market), 'but I wouldn't trade it for anything.'"

I've noticed an increase in simplistic magazine stories extolling the virtues of rural life since September 11, and anecdotal evidence from New York and Boston suggests more urbanites than ever are booking passage to parts unpaved. But the elevation of the back-to-the-lander as a noble post-modern savage has been going on for more than a decade, coinciding with the revelation that big corporations no longer guarantee you a job for life, not to mention health insurance for your wife. This trend reverses the earlier image of the soft-headed country bumpkin, as popularized in '60s TV shows like *Green Acres*. That characterization paralleled the postwar urban migration, when staying down on the farm was what losers did.

At this point the rural writer is supposed to puff up his sunken chest and announce that both of these self-serving stereotypes—the brave back-to-the-lander and the idiotic rube—are hopelessly inaccurate. But the fact is, both ring true, at least as far as they go. I know people in my town who let livestock roam in their homes, like Arnold the Pig on *Green Acres*. But I also know farm folk who wouldn't trade their toil for anything, because fresh snow on a stone-walled pasture before the snowmobiles tear through is grander than any townhouse on Beacon Hill.

One is Nanney, the only person in my town who has appeared on *The Oprah Winfrey Show*, for a segment about women who are living their dreams. This single mother of two boys sells her own handcrafted sweaters out of yarn she produces from her flock. If Nanney had been one of those shepherds in Bethlehem on Christmas Eve, the archangel Gabriel wouldn't have needed to say "Fear not!" When Nanney's house and barn burned to the ground in 1990, she saved her sheep, but little else. Nanney soldiered on, building a new house and a beautiful timber-framed barn.

She wasn't exactly born in a barn. Nanney grew up in a comfortable Massachusetts family with long ties to Maine; her grandfather was a legendary sportsmen's guide in Baxter

State Park, the wild and rugged terminus of the Appalachian Trail in northern Maine. She breezed through Bowdoin in three years before shocking her family by announcing she wanted to be a farmer—and enrolling at The University of Maine for graduate studies in agricultural economics. "My dad said 'What the hell are you thinking?'" she says. "I said 'I'm thinking the world is crashing down, and I want to help break the fall.'"

It's a good thing Oprah wasn't around on the snowy day I dropped by to help Nanney trim sheep hooves. It's messy grunt work, but it's important: if left alone, the hoof grows over onto itself and creates pockets that breed dangerous bacteria. I'd been wanting to learn more about sheep care, and Nanney can always use a hand, so we made a date and met in her sheep shed, surrounded by seventy dark-eyed chaperones.

"The first thing to learn is how to flip a sheep," said Nanney while pivoting a full-grown Dorset around her leg and rolling him over on his backside in seconds. I introduced myself to "Mike" (not his real name) and went to work. "Hmmm, he doesn't want to move," I said to Nanney after about five minutes of pointless manhandling, "and he feels kinda greasy. Is he okay?"

"That's the natural lanolin in his fleece," said Nanney as "Mike" urinated copiously down my pant leg. His bladder now empty, he finally deigned to let me flip him. Using a pair of hoof shears that resembled a rose pruner, I started trimming. The trick, Nanney instructed, is not cutting into the quick, which can't be seen because the hoof is opaque.

I remembered how my cat shrieked when I'd accidentally

clipped into the living quick, and I was terrified of making that mistake on someone else's beloved sheep. As a result, I wasn't cutting nearly enough; Nanney kept coming by and hacking my artful little trims down to nubbins. The first time she cut into the quick, I cringed, and braced for The End of the World as We Know It. "Yikes!" I screamed.

"It's okay," she said calmly, continuing to clip around the bleeding hoof. "It happens. It's really no big deal—like clipping your fingernail a little too short." In fact, the sheep seemed oblivious as the cloudy magenta stream ran down his leg and covered Nanney's hands.

By the end of the day my back was aching, and I don't think I'd been much help to Nanney, having clipped just four sheep. But I learned a lot, and it was the messy kind of lesson that sticks to you, even after you wash the sheep out of your clothes. Nanney would agree. In grad school, her professors urged her to set aside her thesis work (on promoting small-scale agriculture through handcrafts) and just go out and do it. So she did. As if to confirm her decision, the house fire destroyed all her thesis research. She's been farming ever since. I wish I felt as sanguine as she about the future of family farming, or in fact the future of our town.

25

Okay, it's settled. I'm moving back to New York. I've written my last swing-handled basket story for *Martha Stewart Living*. I'm going back to my old job at *People* to write about important stuff, like celebrity pets.

All right, I'll stay. But it's hard to get excited up here in January, now that winter has arrived and the last cluster fly buzzing around my bathroom skylight has finally dropped into the tub. I mean, somewhere in Santa Fe, Julia Roberts is probably cavorting with a Labrador puppy; there's a photo just waiting for a professionally written caption. We pros have to go where the work is, right?

I'm not the only one up here getting antsy. Almost a year has passed (and a lot of rancid air) since Lane filed its application to carve a fifty-six-acre rock quarry out of our town. We whining complainers who believe that the quality of life in our two-hundred-year-old town is more important than cheap asphalt for Wal-Mart parking lots still haven't had the chance to speak up at a public hearing. Modern rural life is endlessly complicated, and this endless fight over land use in a farm town illustrates why.

Several newspapers have characterized our battle as a classic Maine culture clash between "old-timers" and "folks from away"—the tradition-bound versus the *arrivistes*. It makes for a good story; you can picture the crusty local (with a heart of gold, duh) scratching his chin and ending every word in "ayuh," versus the Volvo-driving refugee from Park Slope who feeds deer from her swing-handled basket and respects what her body is telling her.

But the truth, as usual, is less sharply drawn yet more interesting. Knock on any door around here (reporters don't usually do that), and you'll meet quarry opponents whose last names are engraved on the town's Civil War monument. It's not about where you're from.

Locals know that the real conflict is between the good old boys (who come from anywhere) and the rest of us who don't own dump trucks. A leader of the good old boys is Bradley, the gavel-pounding, putty-faced planning board chairman— and the man with the fate of the rock quarry in his hands (for the moment).

I cannot think of a Hollywood character actor who could portray Bradley, although he appears closely related to Jabba the Hut on both sides of his family. His sartorial range runs from blue to green work uniforms, accessorized with clip-on suspenders. But his working-man trappings belie his bourgeois strivings, for Bradley is in fact the local *padrone*, the Big Boss Man. He has attained that status by virtue of owning the used car lot, but over the years he's sold just about everything— land, old coins, anything that opens wallets—and employed just about everyone.

Everyone who owns a dump truck, that is. People in town love to hate him, and the funny thing is, the love part is genuine: Bradley in fact has a good sense of humor, especially about himself, which excuses a lot of his boorishness. His malapropisms (delivered in an impenetrable Maine accent) are legendary, including his reference to the board's regular monthly meeting as "our annual monthly meeting."

Entire myths surround him, and he has attained the status of local anti-hero, like Paul Bunyon in an alternate universe. Bradley once owned a local bar, and one often-repeated story has the regulars voting to ban him from his own saloon.

Not everything about Bradley is entertaining. He once wrote a letter to the local paper, responding to resident complaints about a possibly illegal gravel pit that was keeping babies awake at night:

> I'd much rather hear the groan of a loaded truck coming up the hill than the cries of horses and oxen as they were being beaten trying to haul lumber over the hills—some dying in the process. City folk have no idea and never did. This place didn't come into existence with their arrival.

Many folks in town arrived at a picture of Bradley himself in the lumber wagon, wielding the stick. And of course, if country folk still worked their land with beasts of burden, land use ordinances might not be necessary; generations of horses and oxen could barely keep the woods back from the pastures, much less haul the rock and topsoil off to suburbia. But any reasonable person can see how skidders, excavators, dynamite, and rock crushers can transform the landscape in a week—and make life exquisitely miserable for neighbors.

No, as Bradley wrote, this place didn't come into existence with the arrival of "city folk." But Bradley and his ancestors can't take all the credit. The Indians who inhabited Maine for tens of thousands of years worked this same land with neither horses nor machines.

In his revolutionary 1983 study *Changes in the Land: Indians, Colonists, and the Ecology of New England*, historian William Cronon showed how Native Americans were not the environmental stewards depicted in politically correct fiction. Yet careless as they were in burning forests and depleting soil, they removed from the land only what they needed to survive each season; it took the European economic concept of accumulated wealth to fully transform the landscape.

From the European's perspective, New England's abundant natural resources were a market, not a means of survival or even a romantic wilderness. The region's timber, fir, and fish had almost inestimable value in Europe, yet were virtually free for the taking. Thus by 1800, the primeval forest was gone, and New England was a land of fields and fences.

Today those same economic "rules" make it nearly impossible to be a farmer, and the fields have reverted to forests. But the European legacy of land as a commodity is still going strong, because land is about the only thing rural Mainers have in surplus. Rock quarries are the latest way to turn your land into cash. But to do that, you need to haul it off.

Bradley was only too willing to let that happen. "We're

going to make this easy for you," he told Lane's representatives at the first hearing. That set the stage for a showdown. The real enemy may have been Lane—especially the company's sneering lawyer with a bad haircut, Fast Eddie—but much of our anger was funneled toward poor Bradley, who was in way over his head.

The town's planning board consisted of Bradley and four other guys, some of whom could be found on any given day hanging around Bradley's car lot, shooting the bull. It was a club. Mostly the board rubber-stamped people's camp road plans, or expansions to small-scale gravel pits—modest projects that in aggregate could change the character of a town, but individually drew little attention. Lane was different, a project that promised instant transformation of a landscape, and an endless parade of trucks through town.

The company showed up with an "application" larger than the Queens phone book, and ushered in legions of engineers and hydro-geologists. When our lawyer, Bo, tried to get a word in, Bradley's gavel would come down.

Meanwhile, Bradley wasted hours on procedural trivia. Epochs crawled by, governments fell, and nations formed while Bradley polled board members on available dates for the next annual monthly meeting. He sorted through their litanies of Little League conflicts and vacation schedules while the town's lawyer stared at the ceiling, his expensive clock ticking.

The leaves fell and winter came, and the meetings dragged on. We relished hearings during snowstorms because the Lane crew had to drive all the way from Bangor, an hour and a half away even in good weather. Attendance on both sides dwindled; we all grew impatient, and everyone acted badly at times. One night Vic, our former U.S. Marshal, blew up after Bradley made a crack about "all you retired people movin' up here."

Vic shot up from his chair. "Let me tell you something, pal. I was chasing bad guys all over the world while you were sitting up here on your fat ass!"

Bradley gasped as if hit by a tornado and nearly fell out of his chair, but Vic was just warming up. He proceeded to list in exquisite detail the implements he planned to insert in Bradley's ass, followed by a discussion of how far they would reach. The town library in the next room hadn't closed for the night; through the open door I could see children dropping books and cocking their heads. It was a night best forgotten by all, which will be remembered by everyone.

26

I just spent three weeks playing phone tag with a contractor in California. I didn't want to hire him, just ask him a few questions about a kitchen he built, for an article I was writing in *This Old House*. When I worked at *People* magazine I used to play phone tag with Hollywood stars. But I guess contractors are the movie stars of the new decade.

Actually, contractors are the chefs of the new decade; chefs were the movie stars of the last decade. The gourmet craze peaked, I suppose, with an article in the *New York Times* last summer extolling barnacles as the new fashionable seafood. I had to read the story twice to make sure it wasn't a parody of the paper's trend-conscious foodie section. I've accidentally eaten barnacles at the bottom of some mussel broth, and I've had a few live ones ricochet into my mouth while cleaning sailboat hulls. But as a culinary experience I'd have to rate both cooked and sushi-style "boat warts" about as exciting as fish scales. Clearly, I don't get it.

Anyway, it should perhaps be regarded as a blessing that public fascination has turned from barnacles to kitchen renovation, although the two are plainly related. According to the magazines I write for, the latest must-have kitchen appliance is an eight-burner French-made La Cornue stove with two ovens and a barbecue. Evidently the previous status symbol, a mere six-burner Viking, did not provide enough cooking space for today's divorced parents of 1.5 children. The magazines, not to mention the floorboards, groan under the weight of these obscene extravagances. With all those pots boiling, simmering, reducing, and caramelizing, how do the owners find time to read?

The truth, of course, is that people don't "read" magazines any more than they "cook" eight things at once—a fact also confirmed by the *New York Times*, in a recent article head-lined "Magazines Push Images Over Words." (As I read this article on the Times website, an animated ad for the Microsoft Network popped up, and a rainbow-colored but-terfly floated across the page.) Today's successful magazines are mainly about captions, which seem to be a literary genre for the new millennium.

The other truth is that real people don't own eight-burner La Cornue stoves, which exist primarily in the glossy pages of magazines to convince advertisers that their readers are "upscale."

Advertisers aren't much interested in my corner of Maine, where upscale often means a double-wide trailer. When it comes to fancy cookware, my neighbors are not even in the parking lot, much less the ballpark, although they know better than to eat barnacles. Most of them would agree with author Carolyn Chute *(The Beans of Egypt, Maine)*, who once observed that if Maine wanted to honor genuine Maine food, they should have put macaroni-and-Spam on the license plate instead of a lobster.

I love a steaming dish of homemade macaroni as much as I love lobster, but I do not share Chute's taste for the trashy trappings of rural Maine life. I find trailers and their inevitable accessories—snowmobiles, all-terrain vehicles, and tire piles—a scar on the landscape. I feel guilty about it, because I know that trailers allow poor people to own their own homes, which is to be encouraged. But do they have to be so ugly? Can't some public-spirited architectural initiative come up with a better design for low-income living? Surely vinyl siding, faux plastic shutters and living rooms the width of a traffic lane are not the only solution. When did life become so commoditized that homes built of poisonous crap became acceptable? People of modest means used to live in real (albeit modest) houses made from trees; many were sold as kits by Sears and other catalog companies. What about our society now makes that so impossible?

I suspect our rush to renovate, and add extra bedrooms, bigger stoves, and more Italian terrazzo, is a subconscious reaction to the cheapening of life on the bottom end of society. If they ever did a TV show about our parents' homes, it would be called *This Same Old House.* Their generation lived in the same old house all their lives; they never remodeled kitchens or added new wings, and the stove got replaced only when it broke beyond repair. Sarah's parents still don't have a dishwasher, and they don't care.

I don't have the answer, and no one running for governor this year does either. The best solution will be one that makes sense in the marketplace: something that makes it economically feasible for busy contractors playing phone tag with writers to build quality low-income housing—and makes it affordable for average folks.

That won't help people learn to take care of their property, or take their old tires to the transfer station (which costs just one dollar) instead of piling them in the front yard, or dumping them along a woods road in the middle of the night. (Along my land, worn-out snow tires come up with the fiddleheads every spring.) But the problem is also about money, because poverty is a close cousin to ignorance. If people knew enough to take pride in their plain old untrendy homes, there would be fewer tire piles in my town, and fewer eight-burner stoves in magazines. If we can put a man on the moon and eat barnacles, we can do this.

27

I hear America singeing, burning beef flesh over coals at Acadia National Park. I join America camping, where it goes to get away from itself. Huddling under tarps and waving off insects, Americans dine in fear of rain but fear planes more, so they drive in record numbers to Maine for summer vacation during wartime.

They arrive in their tanks—hulking, fully loaded SUVs with leather seats, CD changers and plastic grills over headlights to protect them from disobedient nature. The license plates are from urban states like New Jersey and Pennsylvania, and some of the plates have Web sites where you can download useful information and possibly buy mugs.

I smell America smoking, because at Blackwoods Campground you still can. They smoke in the stalls of the communal bathrooms, and they smoke on the granite bedrock along the sea and around the campfire where they say "I hate rabbits!" to drive the smoke away.

I see no rabbits, but one evening a snowshoe hare bounds across a camp road in its somber summer coat of brown and gray, which will turn white in winter. Unlike rabbits, hares are born with eyes wide open.

I encounter no raccoons, but I see wartime America vigilant —sleepless campers creeping to toilets with flashlights, brandishing brooms and muttering "goddamn raccoons!" as they pass each other in the dark. Americans like to stay on top of the food chain, and raccoons just don't get it. They have dexterous feet that can untie knots, so flipping open the plastic latch of a Munchmate cooler is not much of a challenge. And they know what coolers are.

Wildlife is an important part of the Acadia experience—especially at the "Acadia Zoo" on Route 3 in Trenton (seven dollars for adults, just past the Acadia Wal-Mart and the Acadia Home Depot), where the sign exclaims YES, WE HAVE A MOOSE! even though moose do not thrive in captivity, which is why you never see moose in real zoos. YES, WE HAVE LOBSTER ROLLS! says the sign outside McDonalds. Yes, yes, a thousand times yes! Say yes to summer in Maine!

I hear America yelling on the summit of Cadillac Mountain (elevation one thousand five hundred thirty feet, highest point on the Atlantic coast and two hundred eighty feet taller than the Empire State Building, again the tallest manmade object on the Atlantic coast). "Hey!" yells a wide lady in orange stretch pants to her husband. "It says this mountain was discovered by some French guy named Cadillac, and he also discovered Detroit! Must be where the car comes from!"

It is indeed a small world when you're yelling down on it from the heights. Cadillac—the General Motors car division, not the French guy—now makes an SUV that you can drive to the summit of Cadillac Mountain.

I smell America sweating because it is so hot on Cadillac Mountain and there is no shade, which is why that French guy named the place *Isle des Monts-deserts*. Stretch fabric is not conducive to exertion, lacking the characteristic of breathability, and the people on leave from their cubicles are weeping like pink soaker hoses. The sweat pools in the fleshy folds under their arms, and cascades from their foreheads onto digital cameras and guide books. This is not what E. B. White once described as "the perspiration of tired horses." This is the virgin sweat of air-conditioned office workers who eat Egg McMuffins.

I hear America parking, which is mostly honking and cursing. Cars were once banned on this island, but they have since made up for lost time. Today SUVs and Winnebagos line the narrow roads, and they are all looking for parking. Want to try Sand Beach on a hot day? Don't go there. Park at Thunder Hole when the tide's coming in? Hey, the Red Sox could win the Series too. It gets ugly and a lot like the real world, which is what happens when the real world comes to Maine.

I watch America sliding, because overpriced water slide parks are required wherever SUVs and Winnebagos gather in the summer. YES! WE WELCOME HUNCHBACKS! Actually the sign says in precise legal terms that persons with back problems should definitely NOT use the water slide. But lawyers aren't selling the tickets here, and at twelve dollars per, it's hard to turn down customers. So a woman who is plainly hunchbacked and possibly retarded is cascading down the slide, her head ricocheting with a thud against every turn of the plastic carom. She struggles dazed and disoriented out of the pool, then slips while walking across a wet foam mat that sends her feet to the sky and her head crashing to the concrete deck. Blood pours from a gash on her ankle. "I think I need help," she says to the teenage "lifeguard," who fumbles through a first-aid kit and replies "Then come over here!"

I listen from my tent as America goes to sleep. I hear car doors slamming, babies crying, dogs barking, radios playing, hatchets chopping, ice cubes rattling, toilets flushing, mosquitoes buzzing, Jiffy Pop popping, and finally rain falling, which inspires much animated shouting and more door slamming. My melons will be happy for rain, and I doze off thinking of my farm, where I can't hear America living. And yes, we have moose.

Other
Annapurnas

(The Fourth Year)

28

Annapurna, to which we had gone, is a treasure on which we should live the rest of our days. With this realization we turn the page: a new life begins. There are other Annapurnas in the lives of men.

—Maurice Herzog, *Annapurna*

My own Annapurna, which forms a constant backdrop to my ever-changing farm, pales in comparison to the 26,504-foot Himalayan peak that Herzog scaled in 1950. It pales in height, to be sure, rising just 880 feet above sea level, not counting trees and give or take a few feet of snow. But where it really falls short is in name, which I am convinced accounts for its lack of notoriety. In the pantheon of Maine mountains, there are mythic-sounding Indian names (Katahdin), geographically descriptive names (Bald Rock), and historic European names (Cadillac). Then there is my mountain, which I now have to tell you is named . . . Patrick Mountain.

Which Patrick scarcely matters. The point is that I gave up a 31st-floor midtown Manhattan office with a view of the Chrysler Building for a view of . . . Patrick Mountain. I have never scaled Patrick Mountain. Who would? What would you announce on descent? "I've just mounted Patrick!" Would Herzog be famous as the author of *Patrick?* "There are other Patricks in the lives of men." It doesn't work.

So it came as a surprise in my town when we learned that in fact, there are people who would like very much to scale our prosaic little mountain. They own cellular phone towers, and they are trying to put one on just about every high piece of ground in the state. Communities across America are belatedly recognizing these "necessities" as a scourge on the visual environment, and it's getting harder for the tower owners to find good locations. So they tend to operate by stealth— creeping into towns and quietly leasing prime locations before any meddling Earth Mothers can raise a stink.

Patrick Mountain is privately owned, and a prime candidate for a cell tower. Fortunately, some astute locals were ahead of the game; earlier this year, thanks to their efforts, we managed to pass a moratorium on all communications towers until a committee can work up some sort of ordinance or standard that will regulate their placement. I expect the tower companies (and some locals) will call us Luddites and invoke the gods of progress and say how much money we tree-huggers are costing average citizens, but then their R&D departments will find a way to make the towers smaller and unobtrusive, and life will go on and cell phones will get cheaper and chirp louder and mountain vistas will be uninterrupted. It's the American way.

Actually, I would consider climbing Patrick Mountain myself, if only to see the view its summit affords of my farm. But Patrick is heavily wooded, and I imagine views up there are scarce. So I leave Patrick to himself as I go about my other Annapurnas, which lately involve going down, not up.

I was trying to dig post holes and couldn't get much deeper than two feet, at which point the ground became so hard that I gave up. Then I bought a book called *Fences for Pasture and Garden*, which said: "Because setting posts is hard work, most amateur fence builders give up long before they get deep enough." Reading between the lines (where invisible type said "Hire a pro, you flaccid fool"), I called my local fence builder.

His name was Jim, and as far as I could tell, his entire torso was one large, darkly tattooed muscle. You could clone him and put John Deere out of business. In fact, Jim had no use for hokum like tractors with three-point augur bits and other fossil-powered methods of setting posts. He did it the old-fashioned way—with a hand digger, an iron chisel, and a jumbo box of Marlboros. The day he showed up, he was having trouble speaking because he'd just lost a front tooth while trying to tug a six-foot chisel out of some rock; the chisel came loose at the wrong time and smashed into his face. Jim had about as much use for dentists as he did tractors. When the tooth finally abscessed, he yanked it out. He looked over my job and pronounced "Piece a' cake!" Except it sounded like "Peeth a' cake!"

Around the same time, on a day of soaking rain, I heard a knock at the door. Under an umbrella stood a little man with an absurdly bad helmet-like wig, and he was holding two eight-by-ten glossy photos of my house that had been taken from an airplane. "Hi, I'm Steve," he said. "We recently took these photos." Then he launched into a sales pitch that included offers of framing, tints and other artistic effects. At first I was annoyed that someone had been buzzing above my house in a plane, snapping photos, and I was glad we don't have a hot tub. But then I had to admire this little guy for his odd enterprise. I wondered how many people buy the unsolicited photos, and how he could possibly profit after deducting the cost of airplane use.

I didn't ask, because I knew I wasn't going to buy any aerial photos of my house. Maybe someday I'll make it to the top of Patrick Mountain.

29

Some people get up in the morning and decide to wash the car. I get up and decide to dig a two-thousand-square-foot farm pond. When you make it your life's goal at age forty-five to resurrect a rundown hundred-and-fifty-acre farm, time is of the essence. I was reminded of this last weekend when the ticket-taker at the Maine Fiber Frolic (an annual sheep fair in Windsor) refused my money, citing the free-seniors policy. "You just need to pay for your daughter," he said, pointing to my age-appropriate wife.

"What a deal," I remarked. "Say, where's the men's room? I need to change my diaper. Can you speak up? I forgot my hearing aid."

The truth is, I wasn't in as big a hurry to dig this pond as *Home* magazine. While in New York I had mentioned the pond idea to an editor at the magazine. I'd wanted to add a pond ever since the day I cut half my lawn without engaging the mower blades on my lawn tractor. I have acres of lawn, and it takes three hours to cut the grass every week—assuming you remember to engage the mower blades. A key principle of many world religions is living in the present, which means never looking back in life. But there are exceptions; had I stopped to glance over my shoulder, I would have noticed that the dandelions behind me were just as tall as the dandelions in front of me. Instead I was living in my head and paying no attention to the mower blades. That was the day I realized that a pond would eliminate vast tracts of grass.

So last week the editor called me back with the urgent assignment: "We *love* the pond story, and we want it for the September issue. How soon can you do it? We'll need to send a photographer up; what's the best hotel? We can budget him for two nights; is that enough time to shoot the whole process? Any chance it could rain?"

Actually, I was counting on rain to fill the pond, but I could tell the editor wasn't interested in details. "I'll see what I can do." I called up my architect friend Jack Silverio. "Jack, I need a good pond man."

"Well, the best landscape designer I know is down in New-castle," said Jack. "Name of George Workman."

I liked the name, and I liked his way of thinking when I reached him on the phone. I told George my plan and about the magazine and the photographer, and he sighed. "Well, that's the McDonalds way of doing it." I liked him even more. I'm embarrassed by people who get enthusiastic when I tell them I write for magazines, because I'd rather be farming or fishing. I always figure that if someone actually cares about magazines, there must be something missing in his life. "Rich people always want instant landscaping," George went on. "Better to go slow, and see what nature wants to happen. But for seventy-five dollars I can come up and give you a one-hour consultation. That might be all you need; for more money I could do some pretty drawings, but it sounds like you can figure this out on your own."

Two weeks later, George showed up on the appointed day, after getting lost and calling from his cell phone twice. I started to wonder about him at that point, because my house is easy to find and I've rehearsed the directions with about a million people before him. When he finally pulled up, I got mildly annoyed as he started advising me on a better way of giving directions to my house—especially as his "improved" version was exactly what I had told him over the phone. I changed the subject and started toward the pond site.

Over the phone, I had envisioned George as a hippie-eco-Birkenstock-type, but he turned out to be a trim, dark-haired guy with a goatee, probably in his late thirties. He chatted about Barcelona and old roses as we walked to the pond site, a low swale at the end of my lawn leading down to a fetid mud pit swarming with blackflies. "Looks like somebody thought of a pond before you," George said.

"Or maybe looking for gravel," I replied. "It's the main source of income around here." George smiled knowingly; as a landscape designer he spends plenty of time with the rubble rousers.

I explained that my pond project faced two primary hurdles: lack of visible water, and lack of visible money. He suggested I could solve both problems if I was willing to take more time. "The cheapest way to build a pond is get a good man with an excavator out here, and just start digging. Dig out the shape you want, and start going down. Dig part of it a few feet below the seasonal water table, so you get some standing water in there, and then wait. Watch it for a year. See if it holds water. See where it drains. If you get lucky, you'll hit a spring; they're all around here. If not, you can use that dug well over there to re-charge it; you'll need about eight feet of water to sustain a true aquatic system. And I'd re-grade this whole lawn down to the pond, to collect the sheet runoff. You can even pipe your rain gutters into it. Then I'd move these lilacs, transplant the crabapples, get rid of that Siberian elm, build a riprap retaining wall over here . . . "

At this point George left his body, which was covered with bloody insect bites, and began hydroplaning across the Pond of Total Renovation, which unlike my own festering tarn has no bottom. Okay, he couldn't have known that I recently spent eight thousand dollars fixing my house foundation. But when he started to tell me all the work I needed to do on my foundation, I growled and said "Don't go there." Still, George was a smart guy and fun to listen to, and he was right about taking time to build a pond. I called back the editor. "I think you should find a nice little koi pond in the suburbs," I said. "My pond is gonna take longer than two days."

Two years later, still no progress. Still haven't found the right man with an excavator. Not that I'm auditioning candidates. The longer I live here, the less goal-oriented I become. When the right guy comes along at the right time, we'll find each other.

30

When *Reader's Digest* flew me down to New York to write about a dog show, I had to laugh. I have been indifferent to dogs since a strange one bit me on the face as a boy. At some point I got over my childhood fear of dogs—except of course for really big ones, black ones of any size, barking or growling ones, medium-sized unleashed ones, little ratty ones, nervous ones, three-legged ones, one-eyed ones, jumping ones, and sleeping ones. I guess I just have a hard time accepting dogs on their own terms.

Zoologically speaking, I know dogs are supposed to barf on the rug, roll in dead animals, and eat their own excrement. I do not question God's plan for these lowly beasts. But on some elemental level, when I see dogs doing the dog-ly arts, I can only imagine how disgusting it would be if a human did that, and then the whole dog thing is a washout for me.

Nonetheless, I spend large portions of my life in the company of dogs, and not just on assignment in Madison Square Garden. For reasons beyond my personal control, I have owned or co-habited with a succession of whippets, setters, and retrievers, and my strolls through the dog show brought back a flood of memories and foul odors. I'm happy to report that competitors from Maine had some of the most interesting species—big, noble sheep dogs and other farm workers—while overly tan folks from icky places like Houston favored pointless, decorative breeds like miniature poodles that eat from smelly little cans and lick your face.

Unfortunately I was with a slightly neurotic New York photographer who liked that kind of dog, and I stood off to the side with my notebook and shuddered while she burned through entire silver mines of film on yapping pooches lick-lick-licking their leather-faced masters. I was embarrassed. I wanted to be home with my family. I even missed our family dog, a seven-year-old golden retriever named Rosie who has barked four times in her life and whom I have never allowed to lick me.

Rosie became an issue in our family this summer, when we finally decided to rent a house in Camden for part of the year. The owner of the house might have done the sensible, normal thing that landlords generally do—ban dogs. But no, she had to make life complicated by allowing dogs, provided the tenant forks over a large deposit and agrees to make good on any canine-induced damage. The house in question was relatively new and featured beautiful wide-pine floors throughout. As it had taken Rosie approximately three hours to lay tapestries of scratch marks across the new pine floors in our own restored farmhouse, we decided reluctantly to give her away.

As it happened, another family at our kids' school was looking for a golden retriever; their own had recently died, apparently before totally destroying their own floors, and they were seeking to get the job finished as quickly as possible. But when it came time to make a decision they seemed to lose interest, so Sarah contacted a golden retriever rescue group in New Hampshire. They promised to find Rosie a good home— easy enough for a purebred with a sweet, gentle personality— and one day last month we loaded sad Rosie, her papers and her food into the car for the three-hour drive.

Five miles from home, Sarah turned to me in tears and said "I don't think I can do this." The kids started bawling and I pulled off the road. "We can try those glue-on nail protectors," she said.

"What happens when she pukes on their rugs?" I countered, pulling the car back onto the road.

"I don't think the rugs in there are so nice," said Sarah, and I pulled over again. We sat there as grapple trucks thundered by on Route 17, trying to remember the floors and the rugs in a house we had only walked through once. "Rosie needs lots of love and attention, and I don't think we have the time to give her that," said Sarah. I put the car into drive.

"We'll take better care of her, Dad," said my son Harper.

"Will you walk her every morning?" asked Sarah.

"I promise," said Harper. I pulled over again, made a U-turn and brought Rosie home. Sarah told the rental agent to draw up the deposit papers, and the kids took Rosie for a run.

But it wasn't over yet. Apparently our school friends were going through as much angst as we were. The following week they called back: "We've decided we'll take Rosie." It seemed like the right thing to do.

We cried when Rosie jumped into the back of their minivan. "You can come and visit her any time," our friends said, and we cried some more. When we moved into the new house and Sarah saw the dog scratches across all the pine floors, she cried a lot.

I was surprised at how much I cared, and still care, about that quiet, smelly old dog. I suppose I don't let myself get close to dogs because dog ownership so often ends badly, or sadly. After spending a year living between the Camden house and our farm, we moved back fulltime to the farm. Now we have a new dog, a Cardigan Corgi. They make great sweaters, I tell people, as Sarah frowns. But if I'm ever forced to attend another dog show, I'll go see the golden retrievers.

31

Time was when your plane descended into San Francisco through a shroud of primeval fog, and it was romantic and made you want to write like Jack London. Today what your plane descends through is mainly smog, which sits like an inland sea over the length of the Silicon Valley, giving perverse new meaning to the song "Do You Know the Way to San Jose?"

The high-tech revolution that transformed Northern California was supposed to be clean. Unlike the pollution-based prosperity of the East, where belching factories vainly turned out products that people wanted to buy, the high-tech economy would be about Ideas. Clever young people would come up with Concepts, which would make Wall Street buy their Stock, which would make everyone fabulously wealthy without slag heaps or conveyor belts. It was all so Green.

But they forgot about the cars those clever young people would drive. The dot-com bubble, it turns out, was filled with carbon monoxide. Now Silicon Valley is L.A. without stars—endless ribbons of eight-lane freeways laid over grids of six-lane boulevards connecting shopping centers, parking lots, and Taco Bell windows. The young people piloting those silver BMWs through the haze look more beaten and worn down than my grandfather did after a lifetime on the Chrysler assembly line.

I was in California to work on a cookbook with two chefs, and a week away from Maine in February was a pleasant enough assignment. My destination was Carmel, an impossibly quaint village at the northern end of Big Sur, far enough south of the Silicon Valley to escape the noxious glare that I had flown into and over. Hovering moodily above a rocky, isolated cove yet a day's drive from Alleged Civilization, Carmel faces many of the same development pressures as coastal Maine. Still, the similarities might be regarded as superficial to someone, like Sarah, who was still in Maine in February.

"Don't sound so cheerful," she said over the phone on the day after I arrived. "It snowed again last night, and my car's stuck in the driveway."

"That's funny," I said, "I was out walking on the beach this morning, and I didn't get stuck at all."

"I'm not laughing."

Then again, she wasn't in Carmel, a place of such studied communal cuteness that I assumed the town's most important electoral office was not mayor (a position once famously held by Clint Eastwood) but designer. In fact, professional gardeners with their trucks full of clippings appeared to outnumber residents. Every bush and tree was pruned into exquisite submission, and the pruning never stopped.

The houses were mostly in what might be called the California Fantasy style—which is to say every style in the book. On a single block you might find a clapboard New England "farmhouse" with moss-covered shake roof; a stuccoed Hansel-and-Gretel cottage professionally "distressed" to look dilapidated; a Victorian manor with gingerbread trim and a slate roof (artfully chipped, of course); and a Prairie-style early Modern mansion by Frank Lloyd Wright, who designed three homes in Carmel. The driveways led to parking garages blasted two stories deep—at three million dollars for a small vacant lot with ocean views, nobody wastes above-ground space on cars. High up in the windows of these zillion-dollar follies, people with tightly stretched faces sweated over computerized exercise bikes. It was like Disneyland, without the fat normal people from Nebraska.

And like Disneyland, Carmel has no street addresses. Houses are identified by names (Lookaway Cottage, etc.) or description ("Third house west of Camino Real on Ninth Street"). At some point the town decided that normal addresses and mailboxes wouldn't be cute enough, so everyone (even Clint) picks up mail at the post office. "You can't believe the hassle getting FedEx here," said my friend Taylor, a part-time Mainer who also lives in Carmel, in a house called Merry Oaks.

One night I decided to walk over to Taylor's place. "Bring a flashlight," he said.

"A flashlight?"

"No street lights in Carmel. Light pollution. People here want to see the stars."

"But not the trees, huh?"

"That's right. If you don't want to bash into one, bring a flashlight."

Not that you could walk around blissfully ignorant in the daytime. One morning I returned from a stroll on the beach with a handful of pebbles for my kids' rock polisher, and my hosts Mark and Clark were mildly shocked. "It depends on the beach," said Clark, "but at some places, you're not allowed to take anything." I felt sheepish about inadvertently breaking local shoreland rules, but I also lamented the efforts of well-meaning nature lovers to turn the natural world into a "don't touch" museum.

I saw pockets of resistance: one morning there was a guy surf-casting off some rocks, the only human besides myself who wasn't jogging. His primal exertions were strangely silhouetted against a '60s Modernist house with a gull-wing roof cantilevered over the Pacific. I clambered out to him. He spoke mostly Spanish, and he was using frozen shrimp to catch sea perch. He opened his cooler and showed me six of the small orange-and-blue fish. They would make a tasty dinner—at a table no doubt many miles from this millionaires' enclave.

Behind us on a knoll overlooking the sea was Tor House, the rambling stone residence (now a museum) built by the great naturalist poet Robinson Jeffers. When Jeffers settled in Carmel in 1914, the place was a barren plateau of scrub oak; now his home sits amid the fantasy mansions of the dot-com crowd. Jeffers wouldn't fit in—not that a poet could afford to buy in Carmel these days. He despised the "civilizing" of California's Big Sur coastline, and he died bitter and isolated in 1962—when the way to San Jose was still a two-lane road.

32

I t was supposed to be a warm weekend and I had to go away yet again, so on Friday afternoon I started bringing the tomato seedlings inside. My greenhouse is not exactly automated, and if I'm not around to open up the vents, it hits one hundred degrees by early morning. That's enough to fry young tomato plants, so into the house they went. Trudging back and forth with arms full of plant trays, I started pondering how to raise a billion dollars to automate my greenhouse, clear land, seed hay, build fencing, raise outbuildings, fill ponds, divert streams, and buy fleets of John Deere vehicles plus a one-horse open sleigh when a voice interrupted my impossible daydream.

"Hey, Max."

From the walkway came the sound of Wesley, our first selectman, and then came his red Tingley dairy boots, clomping around the corner of the greenhouse. Wes sells me loads of manure from his blue-ribbon oxen every spring. It would be easy to make a crack about a politician who literally trades in bullshit, but in Wesley's case it would be wrong. For one thing, Wes insists he's not a politician—arguably true given that the office of first selectman is non-partisan. But mainly it would be wrong because Wes represents everything that can be right about rural citizenship. I love seeing him

around my farm, and I love listening to his wisdom on tractors, or town warrants.

"How are ya, Wes?"

"I'm stuck."

"So vote *maybe*."

"No, I'm stuck in your garden. I backed up too far, and in
she went. It's wetter'n it looks out there."

I went out back and there was his dump truck, listing to
starboard in my melon patch, both sets of rear tires buried to
the axle in spring muck and a load of manure hanging in sus-
pended animation. "Hmmm . . . I don't think my four-
cylinder Ranger can pull that out."

"No, I doubt that," said Wes, scratching his grey beard.
"Can I use your phone?" He went inside to call Triple-A
while I cleaned up in the greenhouse.

The job of small-town selectman is, on the surface at least,
a thankless task—in part because it's not a real job. Our town
pays its first selectman six thousand dollars a year—twice
what the second and third selectmen earn, because he has to
do more paperwork; we're too small to hire a professional
town manager. (Each selectman is sort of like one-third of a
mayor.) For that salary, Wes works at least 20 hours a week,
mostly at night and on weekends. After meetings, he gets to
put away the folding chairs.

The other reason it's thankless is because citizens don't
show up at selectmen's meetings to give standing ovations.
They come to complain—about a noisy neighbor, a stray dog,
a pothole. Selectmen tend to walk around town flinching.

Thus few people want the job, and yet Maine's governing

system gives these minimum-wage local representatives broad power over your life. Still, in towns around New England, more people turn out for presidential elections than to cast their annual selectmen ballots. But a selectman can directly affect issues, like local land use and spending, that have the potential to make your life instantly better—or exquisitely miserable.

If you're lucky, your selectmen will be hardworking semi-retirees like Wes, who used to be a metal worker at Bath Iron Works, where Navy destroyers are built. If you're unlucky, you get people who can't hold down a real job (we've had some of those), or people with glaring personal agendas.

One classic local agenda is a variation on the old Bush Senior mantra "no new taxes"—except on the local level you don't have to read their lips; just read the annual town Tax Collector's Report. The low-tax candidates are usually the ones listed under "Unpaid Balance." Once at town meeting, someone suggested that you couldn't run for selectman until you paid your own property tax, which would have eliminated several perennial candidates. But the low-tax crowd shouted that one down.

Wes pays his property tax and he doesn't have an agenda, other than quietly endeavoring to preserve the town's traditional rural character. He gets re-elected despite well-organized challenges. He's well-liked by the town's old guard, who accept him as one of their own—perhaps because he has a dump truck, even though he's technically from away, having emigrated from distant Massachusetts as a child in the 1950s. And the town's growing ranks of back-to-the-landers appreciate Wes because he doesn't call them "you people" like his brother Doug (our second selectman and a very different person from Wesley), and because he's an organic farmer who sees more in the woods than a quick buck.

Nor does he pass the buck. When the town's conservation committee, on which I serve, wanted to create a small public park out of a vacant lot in the village center, he didn't scowl and complain about how broke the town is; he encouraged us to draw up a plan and seek state funding. Then, after our committee leader Judith got a Gateways grant from Augusta, he pushed the other selectmen into bridge-funding the project until our grant money came through. You couldn't ask for a wiser small-town leader.

There was a time when thoughtful rural men like Wesley could become President—and still make a difference in the small towns they came from. Today of course, Presidents (and Presidential hopefuls) are corporate weenie-heads who pretend to be farmers or ranchers for a few minutes while the cameras are clicking before they go back to their real job—groveling for billions to buy TV ads. Genuine leaders like Wes get stuck in the muck behind my house. I'm actually kind of glad. If Wes were President, I'd have to look somewhere else for bullshit.

33

"Drought Leaves Maine Stoic but Struggling," read the front-page headline in the *New York Times* on March 15. "Drought Leaves Maine Parched and Pissed Off" is more like it, but to make page one of the *Times* you need something a little deeper, something more revelatory of the human condition, something incredibly tired and clichéd. In short, it's a great chance to dust off the old "stoic Mainer" stereotype.

The stoic Mainer was created by the newsmedia and summer people to explain the real Mainer's strange diffidence, which stems from fear and distrust of the unknown. In my corner of the state, many folks wouldn't know a Stoic from a Studebaker, although both sound suspiciously from away—like those chirpy TV newscasters who blather on about what a beautiful day it is when the rest of us are praying for rain. How nice. While you're out on your picnic, can we come over and take a shower?

My one-hundred-eighty-foot drilled well ran dry last August and has since come back, although the water is too sandy to drink or cook with, and my kids' bath looks brown even before they get in. I do wonder what my water will be like by this summer, but I have neighbors who are much worse off. They have shallow dug wells with not much more than a puddle in the bottom. They flush their toilets with a bucket from the rain barrel.

Despite all this angst over water, the *Times* reports that only forty-eight Maine households have received low-interest loans from the U.S. Department of Agriculture to drill new wells, even though many more such loans are available. The reporter cites this statistic as evidence of Maine stoicism. "Rather than complain to the government—or to anyone, for that matter," he writes, "people here seem to be willing to wait out their problems."

Maybe, but the Mainer's aversion to borrowing money is less a measure of fortitude than another variant of distrust—in this case distrust of government, which usually comes around to tell him about some new way he can't be allowed to wreck his own land. Then there's the element of Yankee thrift, which was not invented by the newsmedia. Even "low" interest is, after all, interest—a vaguely suspicious concept that is best reserved for essentials like twenty-four-foot inboard-outboards with deep-V hulls.

Power-boat mania in my town reflects more than blind optimism that the lake will actually be wet this summer. It's another indication that Yankee thrift seems to be going the way of water. One of the largest employers around here is the credit card giant MBNA. It's hard to quibble with a company that gives millions to local schools, parks, and charities while turning chicken pluckers into telephone "sales associates." But it's not impossible to quibble, and here's mine: MBNA and other credit banks profit by encouraging Americans to spend more money than they earn. When that financial house of cards tumbles, it's always the poorer, less educated folks who lose their houses first. (MBNA has lobbied vigorously for laws making it tougher for borrowers to seek bankruptcy relief.)

And besides, they call at supper time.

How did spending become such an obsession in frugal Maine? Our very own Senator Olympia Snowe is proposing a national sales tax holiday to "stimulate" the economy. Implicit in her proposal is the notion championed by Corporate America that if we all just go to the mall and spend more money, life will be better. In fact, as the American Savings Education Council and any financial planner will tell you, the surest way to a lifetime of personal economic security is to desire less, and save more. That doesn't interest Snowe the shopaholic, who believes that buying cool stuff is the solution.

It gets worse: Her proposal calls for reimbursing states billions of dollars in sales tax losses from the federal budget. Well, it doesn't take calculus to see the three-card Monte game here. She would in effect make all taxpayers— including those who choose to save their money—foot the bill for the spenders. That would include residents of New Hampshire, who pay no sales tax anyway but will still have to subsidize the tax "holiday" in other states. It's the sort of "deal" that you'd expect to hear on a late night TV ad—if only it sliced tomatoes.

Mainers may be losing their marbles along with their water, but we are still an eminently practical people. Summer is around the corner, and if stoicism sells more lobster rolls, then so be it.

I had to drill a new well, which cost over five thousand dollars. The old well had basically collapsed in on itself. The new one is four hundred fifty feet deep and provides enough water for house, farm, and a small livestock operation, even during droughts. It was a relief. Few conditions make you feel more like a serf than living in a farmhouse with no water. But I can, however, think of one: selling roadside produce.

34

The minivan from Massachusetts pulled over and a smartly dressed older woman stepped out. My seven-year-old dropped his chalkboard, on which his ten-year-old brother had written ORGANIC BLUEBERRIES $3 PER QUART, and smiled. The two were selling three quarts of blueberries they'd raked and winnowed in our field that morning, and the lady wanted to buy all of them. But when she flashed a ten-dollar bill, they realized they hadn't thought to supply change. I had only a twenty, and as I dug in my pocket for some quarters she handed me the ten and said, "No problem, keep it. Let the boys split the extra dollar."

As she drove off, it dawned on me that she thought I was the one selling blueberries—as in I, a poor sharecropper eking out some extra cash in the summer. She was giving the extra buck to the little darlings for holding the sign, unaware that my entrepreneurial offspring were in fact pocketing the whole ten-spot. Although I personally rake gallons of blueberries in August, I do it for dessert, not money.

I felt like Cinderella. "Wait!" I wanted to yell after her, "I used to be one of you! I used to live in Massachusetts! I once owned a co-op in New York and a subway card! I worked in Rockefeller Center! My tuxedo still fits!" But she was gone. I handed the ten to my kids.

I didn't feel bad for very long, because I'm in the middle of revisions on a cookbook I'm co-writing, and when I get tired of dealing with my New York editors I can go out in my field and rake blueberries—and they can't. On a good day if it's not too hot I can fill up a two-gallon blueberry tray in about half an hour. Then I crank up my old winnower, a sturdy wooden blue-painted contraption the size of a motorcycle, which runs on a primeval two-and-a-quarter-horse Briggs & Stratton that could probably burn whale oil if you ran out of gas.

I'm not sure how old my winnower is, but it was definitely built in the era before product liability lawsuits—which means it is delightfully dangerous, with lots of exposed moving parts and not a single yellow warning sticker in any language. If you needed to invent a machine for the purpose of removing fingers, you could do no better. To start it you wrap an old knotted rope around the flywheel and give it a yank. The motor putt-putt-putts to life and, through a series of rapidly spinning pulleys and belts, motivates two rubber conveyors and a rattling drum fan.

The operative principle of the winnower is wind: As the berries drop off the edge of one conveyor to another about a foot below, the fan sends a blast of air upwards, blowing the leaves and sticks out and away, as the clean berries fall into a tray. It works brilliantly and is always a hit with summer visitors, for whom it invariably inspires one of those Rural Revelations—a moment when people who rarely consider how food gets to the grocery store become aware of a clever solution to an agricultural problem they didn't know existed.

I was pondering society's alienation from food production

as I painted a new blueberry sign for my kids the other day; the chalkboard was too small, and they needed something more permanent. Sign painting is a lot like writing, except faster. When you're guiding a brush full of red enamel around the curve of the letter *S*, you can't just take a break and go clean the refrigerator. I could probably paint *War and Peace* in a couple of weeks.

It takes me a lot longer to help two fine chefs write their cookbook. The editors of this book are really smart Manhattan women who know a lot about French food and maybe even more about what Americans want in a cookbook. These are not bad qualities to have in the editors of your cookbook. But like the rest of the real world, they are so removed from how groceries are grown, slaughtered, processed, and otherwise obtained that I find it hard to believe we share a slot at the top of the same food chain. "Sorry," penciled one of them across a recipe for Herb-Braised Rabbit with Celery Root and Sour Cream Sauce, "3 bottles wine, 2 marinades and 1 line describing cutting off the rabbit's legs—we just can't include this recipe."

Although listed in descending numeric order, their quibbles with this dish are, I suspect, in reverse priority. The three bottles of wine are a small financial setback for the presumably upscale readers of the book. The two marinades represent a larger problem, because what people today have the least of is time. But clearly, the real rub is the rabbit.

I had to think about this for a long time. I had to go out and rake blueberries. And when I came back in, what I finally decided was that it was all a misunderstanding: they think the rabbit is *alive*. Yes, that must be it. They think we're up here in Maine cooking bunnies live, like we do lobsters. And I realized that once I make it clear how we quickly and humanely dispatch all land-based critters before carving them up, the book could include new interpretations of all sorts of classic recipes from rural Maine—Possum Loin in a Raccoon Foot Reduction Sauce, Garden Slug Chowder with Acorn Crisps, Henhouse Floor Pâté . . .

The Arrows Restaurant Cookbook (including the Herb-Braised Rabbit and lots of blueberry recipes) finally came out, to excellent reviews. It even garnered a mention in *Time* magazine. Mark and Clark, my two favorite chefs, might soon star in their own public television show. Out here in the backcountry, our two rabbits (excellent meat varieties) have been spared by my kids. The bunnies survive, the winnower hums, and life is generally good.

35

When Sarah's grandfather Stuart was a young man, he desperately wanted to go to college, but there was no money. So he made a play for the Naval Academy, on the shore of the Chesapeake Bay. Alas, his tall dreams were unmatched by his physical stature, and he came up a quarter-inch short for Annapolis.

Not to be easily outdone, he had friends hang him upside down to stretch, and whack him over the head to raise a welt—resulting in bruised ankles and a headache but no commission. Stuart, who turns ninety-two next month, never did get his higher education, military or otherwise—although he ended up serving in the Army, Navy, and Air Force before enjoying a successful business career and many days navigating the reaches of the Chesapeake in his own sailboats.

With the exception of rock stars, it would be hard to imagine even the pluckiest child of today succeeding to Stuart's degree without a college education. In a corporate society where even secretarial positions require four years of previous dormitory living, the computers that now scan job résumés would instantly shunt a mere high-school graduate's application over to the hod-carrier's guild, where he could expect a long career hauling bricks, and no opportunity to convince anyone in "human resources" why he'd be a great regional sales rep. As someone who worked as a bartender until graduating from college at age thirty, I know the limitations firsthand.

Yet at this point it's hard to know which came first: the need to have a college education to compete in the modern job market, or the need to have modern jobs suited to our legions of college graduates, who may or may not know how to spell but who certainly don't know how to carry a hod full of bricks. Either way, the result has been a further blurring of education and job training, a process that began during the industrial revolution.

There is no natural law that says it must be so. Some seditious educators believe it is their job to mold citizens, not train the corporate worker bees of tomorrow—and let the job market iron itself out. But this view has been so marginalized that today the debate isn't whether taxpayers should be subsidizing corporate job training, but whether seventh-graders in Maine are "responsible" enough to be given laptop computers. The implication is that the machine (designed and manufactured by well-trained corporate worker bees), not the child's mind, is what's fragile.

So this month, seventh-graders across the state will enter public schools and pick up their new laptops, one step better "prepared" (says Governor King) for the future. Of course, beyond the certainty that the future will bring more jobs in cubicles in hermetically sealed office buildings, future technology is hard to pin down, much less prepare for. Nobody was "prepared" for airplanes in 1903. Apple, the maker of

Maine's laptops, just unveiled a revolutionary new version of its operating system that replaces the revolutionary new version of last year.

One thing does appear certain about the future: our economy will rely increasingly on the need for standardized customers. After all, selling the same French fries and blue jeans and laptops with the same marketing campaigns in the same chain stores in the same malls in the same look-alike towns across America requires a certain faith that people everywhere have essentially the same tastes, values, and education. The rush to college, the worship of technology, the obsession with school testing, and the push for academics in kindergarten are all, consciously or not, in the service of standardization.

I was thinking about this the other day while putting up potatoes in my root cellar. I grow ten different types of heirloom potatoes, none of which is found in supermarkets. They range from the purple-skinned giant Caribe to the tiny fingerling Swedish Peanut. Two of my favorites are All Red, which is red all the way through, and the truly weird Rose Finn, which morphs into mutant miniatures of those balloon animals that clowns make. No two are alike, which is rather the point.

Most potatoes grown in America are destined for fast food chains, where standardization is a virtue. According to Eric Schlosser's bestselling book *Fast Food Nation*, the economics of modern potato farming are highly beneficial to the restaurant corporations, which buy frozen fries from processors at about thirty cents a pound and sell them for about six dollars a pound. It doesn't work out so well for the farmers at the bottom of this starchy food chain. In return for investing in expensive high-tech equipment that allows them to create a standardized potato indistinguishable from their neighbor's, potato farmers have surrendered to a commodity market controlled by the buyer. Farmers—sharecroppers, more accurately—receive about *two cents* whenever someone buys a dollar-fifty order of fries. "Independence," as the idea was understood by our founding fathers, has been diluted to mean Fourth-of-July barbecues.

Maine's return on its laptop investment will be, I suspect, equally unbalanced. It would be easy enough to mourn the waste of public money on laptop gadgetry that will be outdated in a few years. But the larger loss cannot be tallied by treasurers.

The laptop tells the child: "Are you sure you want to delete the selected item(s)?"

But the teacher tells the child: "You can delete whatever you want! There is nothing to fear! You can delete cubicles and go fight terrorists! You can delete college and play cello on the beach! You can delete laptops and write a book with a pencil! Stretch yourself and you might even get into the Naval Academy!"

Or you could build a root cellar by hauling your own bricks.

Stuart Baldwin died in his ninety-third year, on June 2, 2003.

36

S tandard Time came as a relief up here, where folks work outdoors, and early. When you labor on your feet all day, you don't go jogging after work and you don't much care how early it gets dark in the evening. But darkness in the morning wears you down when breakfast is at five and work starts at six. (Old-timers eat lunch, which is called dinner, at ten or eleven—and dinner, which is supper, comes at four or maybe five on a real busy day.)

So it's a great, liberating feeling to wake up on that first morning after the time change, and see the dark silhouette of the mountains against the brightening sky at 5:30, instead of 6:30, and you feel like you've been given a gift—except it isn't really a gift because you're just getting back what was rightfully yours and taken from you last April.

Back in the '70s there was a hippie health trend called "biorhythms," which I vaguely remember as having to do with cycles of human biological functions. People around here don't pay much attention to their biorhythms unless they get constipated, which they don't talk about anyway. The subject of biorhythms never comes up at the Union Agway— but anyone in my town could tell you it's damn cold in October before the sun comes up, and it's damn hard to fix a busted barn door hinge in the dark. People were meant to work in the daytime, and to do otherwise throws off your rhythm. Around the Union Agway, people think Daylight Savings Time was invented by flatlanders who work in offices when decent folks are having supper. This is God's Country, they'll tell you, and Standard Time is God's Time—besides which the Bible is quite clear on the subject of messing around with the time of day, they'll add, although the exact passage is never cited.

I had been down to the Agway one Saturday morning before the time change, needing some rabbit cage clips, and then I was over to Rankin's Warehouse in Hope, picking up some landscape fabric. I parked the truck and hopped out. "Be right back," I said to my ten-year-old son Harper, who was reading in the front seat. The guy in the store went out back to cut the fabric while I browsed through the latest issue of *Masonry Professional* magazine. A few minutes later he came in through the front door with a bundle of black fabric and a confused look.

"Where do you want this?" he asked.

"Oh, just put it right in the back of my truck out there."

He looked outside, then back at me like I was crazy. Before he could say anything, I was out the door. My truck was gone. So was Harper, whose entire life was now flashing before me. I stood there like an idiot for a minute, my heart pounding, trying to imagine what might have happened. I generally leave my keys in the truck when running local errands; would someone have stolen my truck and abducted my son from the parking lot of Rankin's Warehouse in Hope, Maine on a Saturday morning? It seemed unlikely, but anything's possible.

I was just about to run in and call the state police when Harper appeared like an apparition where my truck used to be. His face was ashen and I knew I was seeing his ghost. I called out his name—in futility, I expected, having seen too many ghost movies. But then he spoke.

"Dad!"

"Harper! Are you alright?"

"Yeah. The truck went down the hill."

"Down the hill?" I ran over to where he was standing and saw that the edge of the parking lot bordered on a steep, brushy ravine that ran down through a line of trees to an old farmstead about a hundred feet below. It's not the kind of thing you notice when you're parking at a store; you'd have to walk out in front of your car and really look. And when I did look, I saw my truck, down near the bottom of the ravine my son had just climbed out of.

"My God, what happened?"

"I got up to stretch and hit the shift knob," he said. "Then it just started rolling." I must have forgot the parking brake—rhythms off from getting up in the dark for so long, no doubt—and when the standard shift popped into neutral, down she went.

It's every kid's nightmare, or at least it was mine. I used to wake up in a cold sweat from a recurring dream of being trapped in my mom's Chrysler wagon (which had a distinctive pushbutton automatic transmission that everyone briefly thought would be the Next Big Thing) as it rolled over a cliff. I knew that the "P" button meant "Park," and in my dream I would frantically push "P" as the big blue wagon hurtled through the void . . . obviously some abandonment issue going on there.

As for my truck, it didn't look bad—missed a big oak tree by about a foot and seemed okay but for a few scratches. I figured I could get in and drive her right down to the back lawn of that old farm. It wasn't until I fought my way down through the brush that I understood why it hadn't rolled all the way down the hill and into the kitchen of the farmhouse: the entire underbody was resting on a rock retaining wall, and the front wheels were dangling in mid-air. It looked like something from an episode of *Starsky & Hutch*.

Standing around waiting for the tow truck, watching Harper's blond hair sway in the cold wind like a wheat field, I thought how incredibly lucky I was that my truck was pinned on a rock wall at the bottom of a ravine in Hope, Maine.

"Lose something?" said the tow truck guy when he pulled up an hour later.

"No," I said. "No, not really."

37

"A re you from Maine?" asked the new dental hygienist as she stuck a mirror into my tonsils and prodded a cracked molar with a frozen steel pick.

"O."

"I didn't think so. Where'd you grow up?"

"Ih-ih-ch."

"Really, you don't sound Southern."

"O, *Ih*-ih-eh."

"Of course, I can hear the Midwestern accent. Plus you don't have Maine teeth."

She went on to describe Maine teeth as being distinguished primarily by their rarity, followed by a succession of plaques, plagues, abscesses, and pustules. The reasons include non-existent health care, non-fluoridated wells, and non-nutritional diets—the last of which will not come as headline news to anyone who spends much time at rural Maine general stores, where a typical shopping list consists of night crawlers and Ding Dongs. (It's worth noting that even catfish won't touch Ding Dongs.) Nor was it too surprising when a recent study placed Mainers (with a thud) in the chunky category, having an obesity quotient far higher than the national average. Mainers have grown so granite-like, it's a wonder the state doesn't slough off from the Appalachians and sink at high tide.

Yet if you live in Portland, or anywhere on the coast south of Belfast, you probably don't see a lot of fat ladies on lawn tractors; in Maine, lack of visible bone structure is a country thing, where its related problems like diabetes and heart disease are common as cows (which by comparison look increasingly svelte).

Country folk used to eat the best food in America—the freshest eggs with deep yellow yolks, home-cured pork, milk straight from the barn, and of course bushels full of just-picked corn and melons ready to explode. All these vital ingredients were produced a short walk from the kitchen door. City dwellers had museums and conveniences, but they had to settle for second-best in the fresh food department.

Not anymore. Now, if you live in Portland, you can buy seafood caught in the Mediterranean and flown (first class, to judge by the price) overnight to a market on Commercial Wharf. You can get artisanal Romano cheese from Sardinia, morels from Michigan, grass-fed lamb from New Zealand. You can make a multiple-course dinner entirely of *fresh* food from other continents.

Meanwhile, back in the woods, you can hear the cellophane bags getting ripped open at suppertime. We are a divided state in many ways, but the two Maines that I find most remarkable are the one of junk-food fatties and the one of conspicuous epicures. No one, it seems, is eating good, normal food anymore.

How did this happen? A lot of reasons loosely interconnected, I suspect—one of those Conspiracies Where Nobody Is In Charge. Blame our nation's land grant universities and agricultural departments, which operate at the behest of multinational biotech corporations and giant factory farms, for driving families off the land; blame the fast food industry, which markets garbage to children, even in our schools, and while you're at it blame the schools; blame "chefs" like the odious TV huckster Emeril Lagasse, a (hydrogenated) snake oil peddler of junk food in grocery stores; and for good measure blame the Republicans, whose self-determinist dogma and worship of the marketplace has turned basic health care into a business. The list could go on, but there is a more constructive response, and you can find it in the writings of Elizabeth Coblentz.

Coblentz, who died in September, was an Indiana Amish housewife who wrote a syndicated newspaper column for the last ten years of her life. Her column, which was handwritten and mailed in to her editor, was not witty or ironic; she did not surmise or conclude; she merely recounted: "We spent last evening tending to Mae. Mae has been my horse for twenty years. Yesterday she injured her leg while pulling my buggy into town; she twisted her ankle in a rut in the road . . . Ben says she'll probably have to be shot."

Her simple stories of life in the 21st century without cars or electricity touched a nerve, and she became a sort of anti-celebrity for thousands of modern readers; her obituary ran in the *New York Times*. (Although she gave occasional radio interviews, Coblentz would not be photographed or appear on television.)

As might be expected, food occupied a good deal of space in her columns. The Amish are trenchermen—an everyday breakfast at the Coblentz house included "fried eggs and potatoes, scrambled eggs, coffee soup and crackers, cheese, toast, hot peppers, jam, hot pepper butter, butter, fresh strawberries, coffee, and tea." But it turns out that like the rest of America, fewer Amish families are farming. Amish men and women are increasingly employed in factories, or as construction workers, and buying their food at the grocery store on the way home. That has meant, inevitably, the introduction of Pepsi and Jell-O to the Amish diet.

Still, as a whole the Amish eat real food, and lots of it. The best of Coblentz's recipes (along with many of her columns) have just been published in a beautifully photographed book called *The Amish Cook* (Ten Speed Press). Dishes like Cheesy Casserole or Raisin Pie might not impress the truffle oil crowd, but they beat Ding Dongs by a country mile.

I think most Americans—from the gourmet fanatics to the Spaghetti-O set—have lost touch with real cooking, which has been compartmentalized into something you do on Thanksgiving. The lesson from Coblentz is that you don't have to live on a farm, or shop in the Old Port, to eat well every day.

38

The shingled bungalow was dark except for a glow in the kitchen window, from which a figure stared as we crossed the icy driveway to the front door. "Aren't you going to knock?" asked Sarah. It was frigid and the sun was gone already at four-thirty, and our two boys, balancing a tray of gingerbread, were shivering.

"He knows we're here." A moment later the door opened, and Cliff smiled.

The holidays here are still an occasion to go out and visit neighbors you haven't talked to in a year, especially the "shut-ins," to see how they're doing and to realize how much they know about you. "Are you startin' a winery over there?" asked Cliff before I got halfway through the door.

"Something like that," I said. "I'll bring you over a bottle."

"I figured them trellises had to be for grapes or raspberries."

I hadn't seen Cliff for many months, and it was time to catch up. His son lives next door, but since Janet died last year he spends most of his time with the four walls, and he seemed glad for some company. Cliff is like a character from a Grimm's fairy tale, and not just because his narrow, twinkling eyes give him the face of an elf. He was, until age and ailments caught up, a woodsman his whole life—trapper, guide, logger, orchardist, anything to earn money on snowshoes, or in spiked boots.

Cliff's front door opens directly into a living room whose ceiling is so low that I brush my head. The room itself is barely big enough for a couple of chairs and a television; off that, in one direction, is the tiny bedroom, and the other way is the narrow kitchen. The floors are covered in faded, curling linoleum, and the paneled walls decorated in plastic-framed faux paintings of deer. On the night we arrived, the house smelled strongly of grease and game, and I could see a large meat grinder out on the kitchen counter. A black powder musket fitted with a scope leaned in a corner. "You bag a deer?"

"Right out that window," he said, pointing to the back of the kitchen. "Didn't even have to put my boots on." I wasn't sure if that was legal, but the thought of a shut-in firing a scope-sighted musket out the window of his house was a pleasing image, if not one destined for the state's new tourism promotional campaign. ("Maine—Stay for a Spell, but Stay in Your Car.") I looked at my boys. Their jaws were scraping the floor.

"Good thing for me them deer come up outta the woods," said Cliff. "After my bypass and colostomy, it's hard for me to get out there. So I just keep my eye out for 'em in the back window. They usually come up on Sunday, when there's less dump trucks spookin' 'em along the road."

I was pretty sure it was illegal to hunt on Sunday—okay, I was positive—although it might be argued that Cliff was not in fact "hunting." It was more like grocery shopping, which many people now legally do at home, via the Internet. Why should a poor country shut-in be deprived of this modern convenience just because he can't afford a computer? Besides, there are those damn dump trucks, scaring off deer the rest of the week.

No, Cliff is a good steward of his land—he doesn't even own a snowmobile or ATV, much less a dump truck. The deepest cuts he makes are with an orchard lopper, on apple trees he planted decades ago. He pays attention to the seasons and he plants by the moon and he believes old country sayings like the one that warns darkly against a dry December: "Bare Christmas, full graveyards."

Graveyards are about the only places safe from the rubble rousers and their dump trucks, because it's illegal to dig up the dead for gravel. The living have less protection; like most states, Maine spends far more time and money busting scofflaw sportsmen than catching serious environmental violators. If you think an oversize strip mine next to a streambed is more serious than a kid keeping a nine-inch bass, you'd be wrong, based on the state's enforcement priorities.

So you have to protect yourself, alas not with muzzleloaders. After we formed a Land Association in our ongoing fight against Lane, the rubble rousers formed a Rights Association. Which rights are not specified, but apparently not the right to move here: "Some newcomers bring with them rules and regulations inappropriate for a town our size," they wrote in a recent letter that was mailed to everyone in town. "We welcome newcomers but not their baggage."

So far, the newcomers to our town have been folks who want a quiet rural life, albeit one with DSL Internet service. Soon enough will come those looking not for farms but for housing they can no longer afford in southern Maine, and they'll be willing to commute to jobs in Lewiston or even Portland, and they won't want to buy a lot of land—just an acre, with a new vinyl house and a fenced-in yard and neighbors like themselves. That will be the end of open land—for farming or gravel mining—and only regulations can prevent it, but the "rights" advocates don't understand that.

Their anger is the terrified scream of a dying breed, like mastodons in a tar pit. Gentle old-timers like Cliff are also nearing extinction, but Cliff is not afraid of the graveyard. He looks out the window at the bare, frozen grass on Christmas morning, and checks the sky for signs of snow.

39

I 'd hate to be a dung beetle," said Whit, my seven-year-old, the other day. "When they get married, they roll themselves in poop." He had been reading a charming new addition to the juvenile bookshelf entitled *Oh Yuck! The Encyclopedia of Everything Nasty*, the cover of which features a photo of a kid with a finger in his nose up to the first knuckle. The book, significantly enough written by a Cub Scout den mother, promised enlightening information on what my son termed "everything"—acne, eye gunk, pee, pus, scabs, snot, vomit (these words actually appear on the cover), and other effluvia.

It all sounded great, but I really perked up at the mention of an insect named after dung, an important element around our farm. "These dung beetles actually get married?" I asked.

"Of course."

"You mean they exchange vows?"

"No! You know what I mean. They, uh, mate."

"Oh, I see. And they do it rolled up in poop?"

"Yeah. They also *feast* on poop."

This was further evidence of the close relationship between food and sex, but I was otherwise unimpressed. Don't get me wrong, I like bodily emissions as much as the next first-grader, but I'd already had it up to my nose—

measuring by my first knuckle—with disgusting stuff. I had just returned from a seminar on poultry disease at the Maine Agricultural Trades Show. This annual farm event is held at the Augusta Civic Center, a place where Elvis actually performed, and in another life (the life in which he never walked into Sun Records and plunked down four dollars) Elvis would have fit in perfectly among the tractors, hay-balers, and implements for cattle worming, a subject that deserves consideration for the second edition of *Oh Yuck!*

I was there to attend a meeting of the Maine Alternative Poultry Association, primarily out of curiosity; although I was familiar with alternative radio and alternative lifestyles, I had no idea what "alternative poultry" meant. I assumed it referred to pheasants and other exotic game birds, which I am interested in raising, but it turned out to mean an alternative to commercial chicken farming—in other words, free range and organic chickens and turkeys. So there I was in a room with about a hundred small farmers in large dungarees, listening to a lecture by University of Maine veterinarian Michael Opitz and enjoying his slide show of diseased livers, scaly leg mites, and infected feces. The bearded Dr. Opitz seemed like a wise and caring man, but his heavy German accent made him sound (to my Hollywood-addled brain) like Dr. Strangelove—especially when he smirked and said: "Zar iz enough avian influenza virus on a piece of chicken feces ze size of a *penny* to kill vun *million* cheeckens!"

A scary and scaly thought, to be sure, even without the German accent—and I didn't need any more viruses around my farm, thank you: Both my kids had caught the stomach bug and had been "running the stew-master" (a phrase I picked up from *Oh Yuck!*) three nights in a row. This stomach bug is highly contagious, so to protect myself I began washing my hands approximately one hundred times a day and eating attractive looking food that would still look nice when it came back up.

No, I could not afford to get sick and start "buying the Buick" (see *Oh Yuck!* page 189), as I had to drive down to Massachusetts and interview the father-and-son authors of the new book *Keeping Faith* for *People* magazine. In case you haven't been watching *Nightline* or a dozen other TV news/talk shows, *Keeping Faith* is the story of a white, upper-middle-class boomer dad whose prep-school son decides to join the Marines—something very few white, upper-middle-class prep-school kids do these days. But the father's initial embarrassment turns to pride as he watches his son slog through the horrors of boot camp and eventually qualify for a top-secret job. The book has touched a nerve with Americans trying to understand the meaning of service and patriotism in today's wacky world. It also has really colorful passages of Marines vomiting.

This Marine has been embraced by the last two Presidents and the current First Lady. So while learning about poultry parasites and dung beetles, I was also getting calls from a brigadier general at the Pentagon, Bill Clinton's scheduler, and Laura Bush's press representative.

To make matters more complicated, I had decided during the same week to run for third selectman in my town. The election isn't until March 28 but the nomination ballot, which requires 25 legal signatures, is due in early February. So when my phone wasn't ringing and the barf wasn't flying, I was scurrying around town getting autographs. I felt like an alternative chicken with his head cut off, which, after the poultry meeting, I could visualize clearly.

Especially after listening to a lecture on poultry predators by a state wildlife biologist named Henry Hilton, who described a phenomenon called "excess killing." At the seminar, a farmer had raised his hand and wondered what kind of animal might have invaded his chicken run and killed dozens of birds without even bothering to eat them.

"A weasel," replied Hilton matter-of-factly. "Weasels are killing machines," he went on, "and when presented with ready prey, they will keep on killing."

I knew how they felt. As if I didn't have enough on my own plate, I buttonholed Hilton after his talk and told him about the beaver pond in my woods, two acres large with a fifty-foot dam. "It's got everything except beavers," I said. "I think they were trapped out a long time ago, or maybe killed by rampaging weasels. Can the state help me re-introduce them?"

"Absolutely," said Hilton. "We love people like you. We're always looking for good places to put beavers that need to be moved."

He gave me a number to call. It's going to be a busy year.

Man of the People

(The Fifth Year)

40

I can't say what made Madison, Lincoln, or even Hoover turn to politics, but it was probably something larger than a fifty-six-acre strip mine. (Maybe not in the case of Hoover, who was a mining engineer.) At any rate, the strip mine in the woods is where it all began for me.

Almost two years have passed since Lane came to town with its quarry application. To no one's surprise, the planning board finally approved a version of the mine last summer (without the concrete and asphalt plants), and now we are appealing, to the town's appeals board. So is Lane; the company brazenly wants to win back its plants, even though it voluntarily "withdrew" them from the application in order to get the quarry passed. The company's duplicity shocked no one; as its lawyer said from the very beginning, "We're not here to make friends."

In the meantime, this naïve back-to-the-lander, who wanted nothing more than a heap of dung to call his own, has been transformed into an unlikely activist, defender of community rights, and, most recently, candidate for third selectman.

As I write these words it happens to be snowing while the sun is shining, which is pretty much how I feel about the whole thing. I'm not sure what will make me happier on

March 28, 2003—winning or losing. Either way, I'll come out of it a better, if exhausted, man.

Which is not to say I'm kicking back and waiting to see what happens. My town has roughly 1,100 registered voters, about half of whom actually vote. You need about 250 of those votes to become a selectman. It would be hard to imagine people in my town voting for a local candidate they've never met, so if you don't know 250 people, you need to get out and knock on doors.

After living here four years, I figured I personally knew about a hundred people—not enough. So every Saturday I drive around town, visiting voters and handing out flyers that spell out my platform: "A progressive candidate who favors thoughtful planning that allows for traditional land use while protecting the community and the environment from unrestrained development." It sounds straightforward enough, but people have plenty of questions, only some of which can be predicted. "If you're elected, whom will you put on the planning board?" (I had an answer for that one.) "If I vote for you, can I get a sidewalk?" (I hadn't thought about that.)

Some folks invite me in and want to talk for an hour. One older woman kept firing rhetorical questions at me ("Don't we want a town where people can feel safe walking down the street?"), and every time I answered correctly (which is pretty easy with rhetorical questions) she said "Bingo!"

"Bingo!" I made a mental note to go down to the VFW hall on bingo night.

Other voters open their doors a crack and clearly don't want to be bothered. Some seem lonely, others angry, but most are grateful that a candidate cares enough to call on them. Everybody has dogs, and they all bark at you, especially by the end of the day when you smell like every other dog in town. Your car gets stuck in lots of icy driveways, which is where you learn spin control.

I think I have a good chance of winning, but it won't be easy. Unlike many small New England towns that have a hard time mustering any volunteers for local government, my town has seven candidates in the running for three selectman seats, including all the incumbents. The current third selectman, Donnie, is a native son and a career National Guard officer. His family is one of the oldest and most respected in town; he is an honest, intelligent, and conservative man who governs only when necessary. I don't think of this race as anything personal against him—I tell people I'm simply running *for* selectman, not *against* Donnie—but he becomes noticeably cool to me after I announce my candidacy. At any rate, his re-election seems inevitable to many, and I doubt if he campaigns any more actively than he governs.

Even more conservative is my second opponent Christine, a sincere and pleasant young woman who is running, as far as I can tell, on a get-government-off-our-backs platform. She has been endorsed by the rubble rousers. Without a doubt she will draw votes away from the incumbent, and I have encouraged her candidacy.

With all these competing factions and interests, I decided it wouldn't make sense to knock on every door; some people are simply never going to vote for me. I needed a plan. I needed a database. I needed Dave the flag man.

I spent two days in the town office with Dave, who's running for second selectman. Dave lost by eleven votes last year, and he's determined to win this time (He served as selectman in '90s). So the two of us put the whole voter registration roll into a Listmaker data program. We identified who votes and who doesn't, who's likely to support us and who won't, who's gone, who's Green, who's dead, and who's Republican. At home later, I took the list and cross-checked it with the town's 911 road list. I drew a yellow highlight through every household I wanted to visit. Then I grabbed my flyers and hit the road.

A lot of voters wanted to know where I came from, and they didn't mean which side of Davis Stream. I haven't tried to hide the fact that I'm from away, or anything else about who I am. When I was designing my flyer on the computer, I noticed I could manipulate the photo of myself to make me look thinner. I played around with it, briefly admiring the thinner me, then put it back to normal. If I'm going to win, it'll be the real me.

41

CONCOURSE DESIGN PHILOSOPHY

> International Concourse is Atlanta's New Front Door to the World. Passengers going to and from the Concourse will pass through the "Grand Arrival Hall" symbolizing the passing into and out of the City of Atlanta. Ribbons of natural light penetrate the arrival area and add to the excitement of entry.

Only the most earnest Chamber of Commerce intern could fail to laugh at this sign, on display at Atlanta's Hartsfield Airport on March 8, 2003. Although in hindsight September 11 did not change America as much as one might have imagined, one clear casualty of terrorism has been airport boosterism.

Apparently not in Atlanta, however, where the ironies in this breathless announcement appear lost on planners. The writer boldly capitalizes "World," a place our national policy has lately marginalized, and one wonders if the "New Front Door" to this "World" is, like front doors in rural Maine, largely decorative. The Marines, I suspect, will go through the mudroom.

In fact, what travelers will mainly "pass through" in this brave new terminal are batteries of armed guards and metal detectors. And they will be passing through in stocking feet, while their shoes are X-rayed for plastic explosives. Meanwhile, the "excitement of entry" boils down to the decision of a privately owned company with the highest paid pilots in America to route seemingly every flight south of Fairbanks through Atlanta. Every day, some twenty-four hundred planes pass through Hartsfield.

Still, I was prepared to credit Atlanta for attempting to introduce some humanism to what is surely the meanest airport in an increasingly mean country—a noisy, low-slung warren of windowless passages, everything attended by employees (fifty thousand of them, or about thirty-eight times the population of my town) with graduate degrees in surliness. But I was too hungry for charitable thoughts, my trip from Portland to Tucson involving seven hours in the air with no meals.

"So where is the *good* restaurant in this airport?" I wondered aloud. The lady at the information desk scowled at my impertinence and slid into robot speak: "Popeye's and Burger King in Terminal C, Houlihan's in Terminal B . . . "

Okay, so it was going to be like that. I scanned the airport map and settled on a place in a distant terminal called the Jazz Bar, because it wasn't a national chain and because it might actually feature jazz music. Fifteen minutes later, after riding several long, slow escalators *and* an automated train with recorded announcements, I arrived at the Jazz Bar, which was playing Marvin Gaye. I ordered a martini and the stone-faced bartender grunted, then turned his attention to a sinkful of dirty glasses.

Ten minutes later, my drink and the "menu" arrived. The choices of the day were limited and no doubt dictated by the seasonal availability of fresh local ingredients: chicken fingers or nachos. When the bartender handed a slip with my order to a glassy-eyed woman in the corner, she looked annoyed but mustered enough energy to remove a plastic airline meal tray from a cooler and shove it into a microwave. Popeye's was looking better and better. I ordered another martini and asked for extra olives.

Before I could swallow one olive, the flaccid, soggy chicken fingers arrived, accompanied by a sealed plastic tub of "Naturally Fresh Bleu Cheese Dressing." According to the label this dressing, whose ingredients included both sugar and corn syrup as well as "Natural Flavor" but no actual cheese, was "processed by E.F.I., 1000 Naturally Fresh Blvd., Atlanta, GA." I closed my eyes and dreamed of a nice roadkill supper.

A friend in New York asserts it was only a matter of time before I began eating roadkill. "Had to happen," he said when I described the wild turkey I had eagerly prepared for my family in late February, and I suppose he's right. It began with the mail. Walking across the road with the day's bills and catalogs, I noticed the limp turkey on the shoulder. It was a fairly young hen, maybe two years old, still warm, and bleeding from a sharp blow to the ribcage, which was shattered. It had obviously just been hit by a car, but not actually run over. I picked it up by its massive reptilian claws and walked toward the house.

"No!" Sarah was standing in the upstairs bedroom window. "No way, we're not eating roadkill!"

Oh, why not? Wild turkeys are North America's largest game bird and I had always wanted to try one—but as I no longer hunt, I figured I would never get the chance. As a boy I hunted pheasant in Michigan cornfields, and I remembered cleaning and hanging the birds (a process that releases enzymes and tenderizes the flesh), then roasting them in a slow oven and savoring the dark, earthy meat. Animals that feed on wild berries and seeds have far more rich, complex flavors than farm-raised meat (including farm-raised "game" served in restaurants), and most of us rarely, if ever, experience it.

It took half an hour to pluck and gut the bird. At this point Sarah was feeling more comfortable with the idea of a wild turkey dinner, as the dressed bird, which weighed six pounds, was now recognizable as food. But it looked more like a goose than a grocery store turkey—dark and thin, with long legs, a high jutting breastbone and much less meat than those store-bought plumpers. I sealed it carefully in plastic wrap and tucked it in the refrigerator for a few days.

Wild turkeys are incredibly lean, so to avoid cooking them into leather you need to "bard" them, which involves laying sheets of pork fat (or cheesecloth soaked in butter if you prefer) over the breast during roasting. To add even more moisture, I stuffed the bird with a dressing made of wild rice, pecans, and cranberries cooked in maple syrup.

The meat was tender and full of sweet, woodsy flavor, and

my kids thanked the bird for feeding us. With apologies to Atlanta and the food wizards at 1000 Naturally Fresh Boulevard, here was a meal that lived up to its promise: naturally fresh, and fresh off the boulevard.

42

When I showed up at the town office on Friday night to watch the vote count, one of the more vocal rubble rousers glared at my muddy boots. I'd been working in my greenhouse all day, and I hadn't taken off my Tingleys with the steel toes. "If you get elected," he said, "you can't wear them boots in here."

He wasn't worried about mud on the floor. No, his meaning was clear: I was a college boy, a Topsider faker who hadn't earned the right to wear real farm boots around town. I wanted to tell him how my grandfather arrived in this country with just one pair of shoes. I wanted to knock the manure off my boots into his lap, and tell him what he could grow in it. I wanted to ask him if I could wear these boots when I danced on his grave. But I was a politician, so I bit my tongue and smiled. "I didn't know there was a dress code."

The hand count of paper ballots took six women several hours, but I knew I had lost after ten minutes. Some of the women were mouthing the names of the candidates under their breath as they counted, and I didn't hear my name nearly enough times. I lost my first political race to Donnie, the incumbent colonel, during wartime. No surprises there, and Donnie was beaming. I saluted him (figuratively) at the town office when the count ended around eleven o'clock, and I offered him my support in the coming year.

In our three-way race of five hundred nineteen votes, Donnie scored two hundred thirty-nine, winning by a plurality; oddly, my other opponent Christine and myself each got exactly one hundred forty votes, which we laughed about. So I lost by ninety-nine votes, roughly the same as George Bush. (Unfortunately Dave also lost in his run for second selectman, by an even wider margin than the previous year.)

One hundred forty votes might not seem like many, but out here in the backcountry, people don't vote for you unless they know you—and despite the influx of retirees and the organic crowd, it's a rare flatlander who wins public office. When uppity newcomers do cast fate to the wind and run for office here, they typically round up a few dozen votes—close friends and family. That generally embarrasses them enough that they go into hiding for twenty years. For a relative newcomer like myself to get twenty-seven percent of the vote was regarded as quite an accomplishment. My strong showing, way beyond my immediate support base, was directly due to my diligent door-to-door campaigning (five Saturdays from nine to five), and (I believe) my inclusive but progressive stance.

I was peppered with praise at Saturday's open town meeting, and was surprised to find myself enjoying newfound status as a town statesman. Even some of the rubble rousers (some of whom I'd come to appreciate during the campaign) were respectful.

I slept well Friday night, in part because Sarah and I were both getting cold feet about the whole thing, although she was looking forward to becoming Third Lady. When I decided to run I didn't have a lot of work (as in paid work), but in the cyclical nature of these things, I was pretty busy, and getting nervous about finding the time to help run a town and do my work. (The office of third selectman pays three thousand dollars a year, which I was planning to donate to local charities.) In that sense, my respectable loss was a relief.

There's an old gospel song that says, "Every road goes higher and higher." Win or lose, I found running for public office, even in my tiny town, to be an amazingly positive experience. It made me feel proud about citizenship and democracy, and not in an empty, flag-waving way. On a personal (okay, egotistical) level, just walking into the voting booth and seeing my own name on the ballot made it worthwhile. But the real value was in gaining a deeper appreciation of the people who live here (especially the people I don't agree with)—knowledge I hope I can carry forward in community service. Best of all, it wasn't about money. (I spent $15.75 on copying and $83.25 on stamps.)

Presidents used to come from similarly small towns, and get their start on similarly modest campaigns. I wish it still worked that way, because small-town politics teaches you to listen, and not just to voters: during my door-to-door campaign, I became an expert at telling which barking dogs were likely to bite, and which were just glad to see you. Listening is a virtue that seems lost on a lot of today's leaders, who spend most of their time talking into the lens of a TV camera. Maybe that's the way it has to be, but I suspect we'd feel our presidents and prime ministers were more human if they had spent some time in dairy boots, banging on trailer doors.

43

H ello?"
　　　"Hello?"
　　　"This is—"
"—Hello?"
"I can't hear—"
"—Hello?"
"This is Agway."
"Can you hear—"
"—Hello?"
"Your birds are in."
"Hello?"

Telephones up here haven't changed much since the party line days, except where they've changed a lot, so that now you have towns like mine where your neighbor has high-speed DSL Internet service, and your own house still has Dixie cups and string.

I was stewing about my communications problem as I drove down to the Agway store. The poultry order is a rite of spring in the country, and it's changed even less than telephones. As always, you order the birds from Agway, wait three weeks (time to scrub down the henhouse), then go to the store and pick up your chirping box of newly-hatched chicks and ducklings. After a few months of worry and care that includes sleepless nights and battles with foxes and horned owls, you'll have fresh eggs and a freezer full of meat.

Back home, I put the birds in the henhouse and called the phone company. "While you're checking on the static," I asked the customer solutions representative, "can you see if I qualify for DSL yet?"

I'd been thirsting for DSL ever since my neighbor Phil got it last year, but the broadband signal only travels so far, and my house was maddeningly just out of reach. She came back with the bad news: "They've done all the qualifying in our service area, and you're not on the list. It doesn't look like you'll ever get it."

"*Ever?* That's a long time. Are you sure?"

"Well, you're twenty-five thousand feet from the wire station. Eighteen thousand is the current limit. Barring new technology, you won't qualify."

"The new technology is called satellite Internet service," I said, "and I'm calling them this afternoon. And once I get that, I won't need your rusty phone lines anymore; I'll live with my cell phone, which also rings in the henhouse." I went out and checked on the chicks.

The next day, Sharon the Phone Lady showed up, her tool belt bristling with high-tech weaponry. "I'm not supposed to do this," she said conspiratorially, "but I think I can make DSL work for you. I'll have to soup up your wires. Gimme a few days."

So that's how I got DSL, and went from static to streaming video in the time it took for Rhode Island Reds to sprout wing feathers. It was a good week on the farm, for phones and birds.

But then one night, while listening to a live Internet radio stream from Paris, I looked out at the henhouse window, which was glowing red from the heat lamp. It was perfectly normal and implied that the birds were warm and safe, huddled together under the lamp. But for some reason, that night it looked creepy, like something out of a Stephen King novel—maybe a book where barnyard animals turn the tables on their masters. I imagined blood-spattered bib overalls and the anguished cries of farmers being caponized and wormed. My skin crawled, although that could have been from the insipid French pop music streaming through my computer.

Actually, I knew the source of my angst. At dinner that night, my son announced his intention to adopt vegetarianism. As he made this statement while inhaling a hamburger, I naturally inquired if his decision was final.

"Yeah—but just with the animals we raise. I'm not gonna eat our own birds."

I understood. The issue comes up in every farm family. Learning to care for animals that aren't pets requires an emotional detachment that is hard for kids—and even many adults these days, given how few Americans have any experience with farm animals beyond a petting zoo. In my own experience as someone who came to animal husbandry late in life, people who raise (and slaughter) farm animals have more respect for these dignified creatures than most well-meaning (and generally urban) animal defenders, who have never slogged out to the barn in pajamas and rubber boots at three a.m. in a blizzard to check on the goats. And while I respect anyone's personal dietary decision (including my kid's) to abstain from eating meat, I don't view the vegetarian trend, or even the animal-rights crusade, as evidence of man's heightened compassion for lesser creatures, or some greater awareness of the natural world.

On the contrary, I see it as a manifestation of contemporary affluence. Regardless of one's personal feelings on the subject of killing animals for food, only a self-contented and well-fed society could afford the luxury of abstaining from an efficient source of protein that humans are biologically qualified to eat. Before grocery stores, you ate whatever you had on the farm. And in January when the chicken stopped laying eggs, you ate the chicken. Chopping the head off a bird you've raised was a distasteful task made considerably easier by the wails of hungry children.

So today we can listen to French radio stations without going to France, and we can eat eggs without knowing what happens to the old hens. Is that progress? I don't know, but by moving to rural Maine I decided, in effect, that raising my own chickens was more important than broadband Internet service. This week I got both, and I guess I'd have to call that progress. But I also know that it's hard to look at those cute little chicks and ducklings and think about the day when I'll be slaughtering them. This is a sadness one lives with, like so many other losses in the cycle of life and death.

I went out to the henhouse that night and sat for a long time, watching the birds dart around under the infrared heat lamp. And when I went back inside, the red light had burned into my retinas so the normal lights of the house looked blue—weirdly, intensely blue—and it was a long time before I could close my eyes and fall asleep.

44

Anyone seeking to re-live a century's worth of boyhood in one summer is urged to hop on his Schwinn Racer, pedal down to the nearest bookstore, and pick up a copy of *The American Boy's Handy Book*. Or you could snoop around your eleven-year-old boy's room and dig up his own dog-eared copy, being mindful of the spring snares, mole traps, and blow guns he has doubtless fashioned according to the book's detailed instructions.

You've got a jackknife, haven't you? Good, because you'll need it. The *Handy Book*, as its name only obliquely suggests, is a four-hundred-forty-four-page compendium of incredibly dangerous stuff that boys can carve, nail, and assemble on their own—from working crossbows to "war kites" bristling with shards of glass. It's a mother's worst nightmare, and in fact you could lose an eye just looking at this book, which is why boys across America are wearing it thin again.

I say again because the book was first published in 1882 by Daniel Carter Beard, an Ohio writer and illustrator. Beard, a friend of Mark Twain and a founder of the Boy Scouts of America, set out to preserve the pastimes of his own rural boyhood for future generations of lads. He succeeded beyond anyone's wildest dreams, thanks in part to a centennial re-issue by the David R. Godine company of New Hampshire. The modern edition wisely preserves the original text, design, and illustrations, however politically incorrect or inscrutable ("How to Make a Horse-Hair Watch-Guard"), and this unlikely bestseller has now gone into dozens of printings.

Yet as I scan through this entertaining manual, I find it hard to believe that many of today's boys are actually making this stuff. Apart from the antiquated materials—whalebone springs, barrel heads—for which substitutions could presumably be found, countless projects throughout the book are now plainly illegal. The chapter called "Practical Taxidermy for Boys" is perhaps the most impractical of all—requiring arsenic powder (which the book suggests any druggist will be happy to procure for a boy) as well as the dispatch of protected wildlife:

> Let us suppose an owl has been lowering around suspiciously near the pigeon house or chicken coop, and that you have shot the rascal. Do not throw him away. What a splendid ornament he will make for the library!

It is difficult to know which is sadder: the prospect of savage boys shooting owls, or the realization that savage boys are no longer allowed to shoot owls. Such are the complex issues raised by this deceptively simple book.

It's also a lot of fun to read. On the subject of backyard snow sculptures, Beard drolly writes: "It is very seldom that pigs are sculptured in marble or cast in bronze, and it would be well to make some of snow, so as to have statues not likely to be found elsewhere." And in contrast to modern "how-to" books and articles, which begin by explaining the difference between a nail and a screw, Beard confidently presumes intelligence in his young readers: "There can be but few boys who are not familiar with that large and useful tribe of flat-bottomed, perpendicular-sided boats called 'scows.'"

As it happened, I was reading how to make a scow in the *Handy Book* when a knock came at my door last week. There stood Travis, a young man of about twenty whom I recognized from selectmen meetings as the organizer of a local group trying to forge an ATV trail through town. His idea is to provide riders of these terrifying machines, which can go one hundred miles per hour through the woods, with a sanctioned place to ride—implying that such a trail will keep them from tearing across the land unfettered, trampling blueberry fields and churning the soil.

ATV clubs and trails are a growing trend in Maine, as riders seek to legitimize the "sport" much as snowmobile riders have. But snowmobiles travel over frozen ground, and while they can destroy young fruit trees and other growth, they don't impact the soil. So it's been harder for ATV clubs to gain access to land, as Travis was about to find out.

He greeted me politely and whipped out a tax map of the town. Travis had the paunchy, sallow look of someone who watches a lot of TV, and he reminded me of those slow-moving teenagers who don't know how to count change at the movie theater concession stand. "We're trying to connect the trail here through the Allen blueberry land, to get over to the mountain," he said, jabbing a fat finger across the map, "and we were hoping we could go through your land here."

I pictured my two svelte young boys, off in the woods with their jackknives gathering saplings to make whip-bows from the *Handy Book*, as ATVs zoomed past them, leaving a trail of empty Bud cans. "I'm sorry, I can't allow it," I said. "I don't think those machines belong in the woods, but you're welcome to hike or snowshoe on my land any time."

Travis looked at me like I had suggested he drink jet fuel, then recovered enough to thank me anyway. "Just so you know," he added, "we did get permission from Clyde to ride along the edge of his hayfield over there. Just wanted to let you know."

This was troubling news. A low stone wall separating my land from Clyde and Harriet's hayfield was about a hundred feet from my door. The next morning, I pulled into their driveway. Harriet came to the door, smiling. She was born in 1924 in that very house, where she had lived all her life. Clyde and Harriet spend winters in Florida, and we don't see them much. I got right to the point: "As your neighbor, I'm hoping you'll reconsider that ATV trail."

Harriet's smile faded, and she glared at me suspiciously. "Why?"

"Well, I know it's your land and all, but that trail would actually be much closer to my house than yours. I'm worried about the noise, but I'm also worried about my kids' safety."

"How many kids do you have?"

"Two boys, eight and eleven."

"We raised eight boys and one girl in this house," she said sternly, "and we never imposed them on anybody else."

In other words, your kids are not my problem. If you don't

like what we do on our land, you can move. She went on: "We have always shared our land. We're from the old school—live and let live."

I wondered what old school had ATVs tearing around the campus day and night. It would be one thing if Clyde and Harriet enjoyed ATVs themselves, but at their age that went without saying. Even under Harriet's "old school" rules, I couldn't understand why it would be more important to let unknown strangers create a nuisance than to care about the safety and comfort of a family living next door. But in rural Maine, the gospel of "live and let live" transcends mere logic, and prohibits reasoned discussion.

In the preface to his *Handy Book*, Beard writes:

> The author would . . . suggest to parents and guardians that money spent on fancy sporting apparatus, toys, etc., would be better spent on tools and appliances.
>
> Let boys *make their own kites and bows and arrows* [his italics]; they will find a double pleasure in them, and value them accordingly, to say nothing of the education involved in the successful construction of their home-made playthings.

What Beard meant by "fancy sporting apparatus" in 1882 one can only guess—perhaps a tennis racket. Certainly he could not have envisioned ATVs, much less considered them suitable for children. One can only understand ATVs as a crude form of power. People who feel every aspect of their lives controlled by some higher authority—the boss, the bank, the oil company—can rev up one of these machines and do something for themselves.

And increasingly, the riders are young. Nationwide, fourteen percent of ATV riders are kids under age sixteen; over the last twenty years nearly two thousand of them were killed while riding. Beyond that immediate sadness is a subtler tragedy, and a long-term problem: children who only experience the woods at ninety miles an hour miss out on perhaps the greatest joy of childhood—discovering the natural world on its own terms. Later, as adults, they are the least likely citizens to respect the environment. Breaking this cycle of ignorance will take more than teaching kids to make scows, but scows are a start.

Luckily enough, the manager of the commercial blueberry field across from my property decided not to let the ATV club ride on his land. ATVs have been destroying blueberry fields, he told me, and he resented the implied blackmail of the club's offer—give us a sanctioned place to ride or we can't control what happens. His refusal to play along threw a wrench into the whole trail network, including the plan for a route along Clyde and Harriet's hayfield, and I have neither heard nor seen an ATV since. Nor have I spoken to my neighbors.

45

As further evidence that location is everything, I direct you to an article in the July 6, 2003 *New York Times* headlined "$75 Rental in Hamptons (Tiny and Organic)." It seems that the ritzy Long Island beach town of East Hampton, which once grew potatoes but now grows mansions for media "personalities" with names like Faith Popcorn, is trying to protect one of its last remaining open fields. The town bought the land to prevent development and is now allowing anyone to rent a twenty-foot-square patch of the field for just $75 a year—so long as they "farm" the plot without chemicals or pesticides.

Ms. Popcorn took out a rental, according to the article, with the intention of teaching her five-year-old adopted Chinese daughter about bok choy and other Asian staples. "She's going to plant, reap and sell it at the farm stand," said Popcorn. In fact, the article goes on, the girl's plot is being tended by a professional horticulturalist named Fusae Shigezawa, along with landscape designer Fred Garofalo, a purveyor of trendy organic compost. Presumably Popcorn will hire migrant laborers at harvest time, for the full immersion in today's farm economy.

Life is less vicarious on my own plot, although I'd put my compost up against any designer brand. True, particularly onerous chores like cesspool draining can always be handed down to offspring, and there's no time like tomorrow when it comes to manure management. But when corn needs planting, who you gonna call? No one. We just walk through the field with a three-foot piece of plastic pipe, dropping kernels from apron pockets every four inches through the pipe into the ground (a trick I learned from my neighbor Cliff). As for our potatoes, when the beetles arrive in July we cruise the rows, smushing the little buggers between our fingers and watching them explode like bright orange pustules. When we need a chicken for dinner, we sharpen a knife and head to the henhouse. And when we gather lettuce for supper, we wash our hands well, and eat from our labor in the summer of 2003.

A typical summer day begins around five-thirty. First you go out and water the ducks and chickens, making sure to wipe yesterday's slime off the waterer. You need to make sure the heat lamp over the baby guinea hens (they're called keets) isn't too close, especially if it feels like a hot day coming. You need to open a few windows in there, which you closed the night before to keep the chill off the keets. You fill up the various feeders. You go out in the yard and fill the duck pool, which will be a mud bath in an hour once the big Pekins get in. Then you need to water all the potted plants. Then you head to the garden before it starts getting hot, to weed a few beds and pull suckers off the tomatoes. Then you start the day's bug watch, checking for slugs on the lettuce and flea beetles on the spinach and corn borers on the corn and cutworms on the broccoli and Japanese beetles on the green beans and cucumber beetles on the cucumbers and squash bugs on the pumpkins. Then you start watering, first the pumpkins by hand with a long hose, then the melons and row crops by drip irrigation, then the lettuce and greens with the overhead sprinkler. You space it out so your well doesn't run dry, so basically you're dealing with the watering all day when it's hot and dry. In the meantime you go inside, sit down at the computer and start writing until you get hungry, which gives you a good excuse to stop writing. But then you remember it's Wednesday, so you load up all the trash and head for the dump. And by then you're halfway to Rockland so you might as well go run some errands, and on the way home, if you remembered to bring your empty milk bottles, you stop at the neighbor's house because it's milking day and she'll have fresh milk for you, unless her cow is about to deliver a calf in which case she's not milking, if only you'd known when you were at the grocery store in Rockland because now you're out of milk. You get home, unload groceries, head out to the garden, look around and think of what to pick for supper. The peas look swell, let's use those. Here's some sorrel the ducks haven't eaten, and we need to cut that parsley back anyway. No tomatoes yet, but we still have canned from last year. Still a few heads of garlic left from last fall; the new crop won't be ready to pull for another month. Check voicemail. Check e-mail. Call the editor who needs a revision by Friday. After supper (pasta with homemade tomato sauce, sorrel salad, buttered peas with parsley) there's always a project. The paint under the eaves is peeling off in sheets. If I wait another year, maybe I won't have to scrape at all. Around dusk you go check on the birds, making sure to lower the heat lamp and shut the windows. You finally collapse into bed around ten.

It's a good sort of summer, in an old-fashioned way, but I admit to sometimes wishing my summer pleasures could be a bit more vicarious. I don't want a Japanese gardener to tend my bok choy, but when I go into Camden and see chattering tourists mounting the gangplanks of schooners, I feel like Nino Manfredi in that great Italian film *Bread and Chocolate*, covered with feathers and gazing out of the chicken coop at the impossibly beautiful Swiss teenagers skinny-dipping in a lake. Maybe next summer I'll do a smaller garden. Maybe next summer I'll go jump in a lake, covered with feathers.

46

In the year I was born, 1957, the tax assessor compiled a list of private property in this town. The Soviet Union had just launched a dog into outer space, and officials here were counting chickens on the ground (fifty-six thousand six hundred domestic fowl to be precise, valued at seventeen thousand seven hundred seventy-five dollars). As dogs account for more chicken deaths than all other predators combined, this was a step in the right direction—or an exercise in futility that Camus, who won the Nobel Prize for literature that year, might have appreciated. At any rate the list, published in that year's town report, contained nothing that might have seemed strange to a medieval serf—except for one addendum at the bottom: one hundred sixty-one radios and TVs.

Although I personally own six times more domestic fowl (twenty-three broilers, eleven layers, nine guinea hens and five ducks) than radios and TVs (two boom boxes, two clock radios, two car radios, one stereo receiver, one TV), I have no doubt there are more than one hundred sixty-one radios and TVs in my town today, and considerably fewer than fifty-six thousand six hundred domestic fowl. Still, just about everybody around here produces some of their own food, if only a few August tomato plants, which sets us apart from the mainstream.

I had reason to ponder this last week, when our family took in a disadvantaged child as part of the Camden to Camden Project. This worthy program brings kids from Camden, New Jersey (a rundown city just across the Delaware River from Philadelphia) to Camden, Maine for ten days of summer fun and a chance to experience something completely different.

Our boarder was an eleven-year-old Puerto Rican girl named Felicia, and her shyness was agonizing; even after a few days it was difficult to coax a head nod, much less a yes or no reply to basic queries. But she was polite, helpful, and eager to learn. After watching Sarah knitting a sock, Felicia picked up the needles and was soon mastering the craft.

She was less curious about our food. Organizers of the program warn host families that these kids are accustomed to what they call a "high-carbohydrate diet"—a polite way of saying fast food and junk food, much of it subsidized by taxpayers at the school cafeteria. "Be flexible," they advise—a polite way of saying don't assume that the delicious and healthful homemade dinners you prepare will be appreciated by your guest.

That turned out to be an understatement. "Flexible" is a relative term, and while I did not intend to serve actual fast food in our home, I was prepared to cook homemade meals that resembled fast food: homemade pizza, homemade fried chicken, homemade burgers on the grill, and so on. Those kind of meals are surefire hits with my own kids, who are also picky eaters. But my kids almost never get food from drive-up windows; Felicia, on the other hand, turned out to be an Escoffier of assembly-line cuisine. There was no fooling her with a home-cooked hamburger; lacking the genuine processed article and foil wrapping, she poked listlessly at the bun.

Sadder still was her reaction to real vegetables from our garden. She cheerfully helped trim a bowl of fresh-picked green beans but would not dare to taste one. I don't think she had ever seen a bean before. It may as well have been a deadly triffid from *Star Trek*. The first tomatoes of August, which my kids anticipate like Christmas, also drew a blank stare.

Feeding Felicia made me wonder if it would be possible, in twenty-first-century America, to live for an entire year on nothing but your own food. This was actually a book idea that I'd been nourishing for a few years, inspired by the fact that our house is more than twenty miles from a grocery store. Living well, entirely off our land, sounded appealing, but when we really started to think about it, all sorts of considerations came to mind. "What about toilet paper?" asked Sarah. A good question—and one that I wouldn't have considered until sitting on the toilet with no roll. We decided we could go to the grocery store for household items, although we would try to make our own cleaning supplies whenever possible. But the rule would be no *food* from the grocery store.

I asked my eleven-year-old what he would miss most from the store. "Turkey tenders," he said—reminding me that some processed food does creep into our diet.

Then I started thinking about basic foodstuffs that, like most people, we take for granted. We could easily make our own bread, but where would the flour come from? I'd have to grow wheat. What about sugar? We could make maple sugar from our trees. Rice would be harder; it thrives in warmer latitudes, although the Japanese grow it on the island of Hokkaido, which has a very cold climate. Out of the question would be citrus, a major sacrifice, unless I could coax a potted dwarf lemon tree in my greenhouse. It made me realize how much food comes from far away, even when you grow your own.

What about dairy? We'd have to get a cow, which means we would need good fencing. Another consideration was alcohol. (The plan was to live *well* off our own land.) I can make my own wine from my grapes and blueberries, as well as press my apples into hard cider, so that wouldn't be too difficult.

My reverie was interrupted by the arrival of Sarah's sister Liz, who lives in a nearby town. "Hey, Max, there's a buffalo in your road."

I was pretty sure I had heard her correctly, yet confirmation seemed in order. "A buffalo?"

"Yeah. Walking down the road."

"Like a bison?"

"Definitely one or the other."

I hopped in my truck. Half a mile away, a huddle of cars lined the shoulder. People were crossing the road and heading into Elden Bartlett's hayfield. Back in the high mowing was a genuine buffalo, contentedly munching away. I drove home and called Leo, the town's animal control officer. "I'm on vacation," he growled. "Call Wesley."

I dialed the first selectman and gave him the news. Wes knows everyone, so I wasn't too surprised when he said he knew whose buffalo was loose. Apparently some guy in the next town raises them for meat; they'd gotten out before. He'd take care of it. I hung up. Sarah came downstairs. "We've got a problem," she said. "Felicia locked herself in the bathroom and can't get out."

"Oh shit." Our upstairs bathroom door has an antique brass latch set with a funky skeleton key I got from Ken Spahr's shop that isn't quite the right match for the lock; as a result, it's much easier to lock than to unlock. When Felicia arrived, we instructed her not to lock the door. "If it's closed, no one will come in," we promised. But a young girl in a strange house full of men and boys surely felt more comfortable behind a locked bathroom door, and now the poor kid was stuck. The one window in there is a skylight; the door is the only way out.

"Can you turn the key?" I asked her.

The usual silence.

"Felicia?"

I heard a sound and looked down. From the crack below the door emerged the skeleton key. It was broken off. I could see through the keyhole that the other half was still jammed into the lock. "Oh fuck!," I said without thinking. Sarah glared at me. I glared back. A year earlier, I had spent weeks renovating that door and three others—stripping layers of lead paint, patching holes, researching historic paint colors, scavenging authentic old hinges and even vintage screws from junk shops all over the state. I went downstairs and got my crowbar.

Good carpenters, the kind who can carefully rebuild a shredded antique door, are busy these days. It took almost a year (and a hundred ninety-five dollars) to get that door fixed. As I was brushing on the last coat of paint, I thought about poor Felicia. I hoped her terrifying experience hadn't soured her completely on the Camden to Camden Project, although I would understand if she vowed never to set foot in our own house again, much less our upstairs bathroom. So it came as a surprise to learn from the program organizers that Felicia was not only returning next summer but had requested to stay with us.

47

D id you mean Linda Linda?"

No, I meant Lipua-Lipua, which is exactly what I had typed into the search engine. I was testing the limits of the web-based Apple iTunes Music Store, trying to find recordings by a seminal African soukous orchestra from the 1960s. Actually, the limits were pretty easy to find. When I typed in "soukous" it said "Did you mean houmous?"

Okay, if there was to be no soukous, why not a little houmous? I clicked on houmous and was transported to a song called "Post Houmous" by the Dover, England electronic group Morcheeba, and it was actually pretty good, if nothing like soukous, so there you have it. Thinking maybe iTunes was strong on Brit provincials, I typed in the Manchester, England group Herman's Hermits, which had eighteen Top 40 hits from 1964 to 68.

"Did you mean Hermanas Hermanas?"

Well, maybe I did . . . but it was another reminder that we live in an age of diminished expectations—or did I mean Expectorate Expectorate, which is what I would like to do on the graves of Delta Airlines and a few other companies with whom I have recently had (non-consensual) customer relations.

My Delta Hair Day began at the LaGuardia ticket

counter, returning home from a trip to New York. The agent was doing even more typing than usual, and I was getting nervous. Sure enough, she finally announced without expression, "I don't seem to have you on this flight."

I checked my itinerary again. It was for today's date.

"Ah, here's the problem," she said. "This reservation is for today of next year."

"Next *year?*"

"Yes."

"Well that's a mistake. I flew down from Portland three days ago. As you can see from my hotel reservation, this was a three-day trip."

"Nevertheless, the return ticket is for next year."

"That's a long wait. Can I get an in-flight magazine?"

"I do have one open seat on today's plane, but it *will* cost you seventy-five dollars." Her emphasis on *will* was preemptive, implying that protest would be futile and possibly a violation of Homeland Security.

"Seventy-five dollars?"

"There is a seventy-five dollar penalty for any change on the return leg of this ticket," she said impatiently.

"But this is obviously an error. It's not even *my* error. I mean, it's not like I just decided to come home a year early."

"I'm sorry, sir."

"Did you mean 'Bend over and prepare to receive this propeller, which for your safety and convenience has been dipped in hot tar?'"

I didn't say that. Even though her apology had the gravity of a gluon, like all Americans I have been trained to surrender my credit card and lie prostrate whenever someone in the "service" sector apologizes. It's a sorry state indeed that this corporate crockery passes for service, and even sadder that this is what Americans who haven't lost their jobs primarily do for a living.

You might think small towns are sheltered from the service-industry scourge and the real world where nothing means what it really means, but folks around here who used to pluck chickens for a living now work for the credit-card bank MBNA, selling debt over the telephone. You could argue quite convincingly that telephone "service" is a better job than chicken plucking, and not just from the chickens' point of view, but still something has been lost in the transition. I won't go so far as to suggest that's why I pluck my own chickens out here, but the fact is I do, and now I have two pigs, which has really put me in touch with my inner groveler, which in a roundabout way helps me adjust to our new service economy.

What I mean is, pigs are a lot like many Americans—fat, pink-skinned, prone to sunburn, and relatively new to this continent, having arrived with the Spanish conquistadores. Like telemarketers, they spend most of their time in small cubicles; in fact, grocery-store pork comes from antibiotic-laced animals that literally have never been outdoors. Primeval pigs, by contrast, were hardy creatures that roamed the forest, groveled in the dirt and required no medication. They used their powerful snouts to find roots and bugs, and their well-developed brains to set traps for other animals. But generations of breeding for mass production have turned these noble animals of the woods into pasty-faced hypochondriacs.

My pigs are as pasty as any airline clerk, but at least they live outside where they grovel with glee, uprooting entire trees within their pen. It could be that people, who once lived in the forest and foraged for food, also retain some primeval need to grovel—one that is met in today's society by our legions of corporate "service" employees, who stand ready to dish out a pail of slop.

48

The inevitable cold snap that finally stilled the crickets up here came on the heels of another moment of chilling quiet—news of author George Plimpton's sudden death on September 25. I had spent a good part of the past year editing a book by George—his last, it turned out—and his demise would have struck me hard in any season, but the melancholy of impending fall seemed to make it somehow sadder.

I'd been hired by Will Balliett of Avalon Publishing Group to edit a series of adult biographies that Avalon was producing for a British publisher and the A&E cable network. Plimpton had signed on to write a book about Ernest Shackleton, the Antarctic explorer whose survival odyssey in 1915–1916 has threatened to become an entire new branch of the media business. Exactly what George—whose previous books like *Paper Lion* and *The Bogey Man* were all pointedly original—planned to bring to the groaning Shackleton bookshelf was unclear.* As time went on, it became obvious that he had no clue either, though he did harbor a desire to visit Antarctica and possibly to write an additional book about penguins.

---

*Upon reading this, my editor Mr. Balliett points out that the pairing had a certain logic, at least at first blush: both Plimpton and Shackleton were self-created aristocrats with a penchant for high adventure.

The first sign of trouble came during a December 2001 phone call. George was at first delightful, chatting away and expounding in that aristocratic lockjaw about penguins and his upcoming trip to Antarctica. But when I reminded him that his manuscript was due in six months, the chatter ground to a halt. "Well, that's simply not possible," he intoned. "Why, Balzac and all his assistants couldn't write a book that fast."

I shifted instead to a discussion of the book's theme and organization, and things got worse. George admitted that he didn't know what he was going to say about Shackleton, but he was quite certain he could not write a conventional biography. Since a conventional biography was more or less what the publisher had in mind, this was going to be tricky.

Down in New York, Will, a man of formidable charm and tact, kept up the pressure during a series of lunches with George at the Century Club, the literary hangout for Manhattan writers of a certain age and a purveyor of legendarily excremental cuisine. Highly favorable to writers on deadline is the club's quaint rule forbidding business papers at tables—a rule enforced with enthusiasm by the club's nonagenarian waiters, who may be deaf to requests for more wine but who can detect the click of a briefcase latch from across the room.

In March 2002, George still had no outline, much less a coherent concept for the book. "I'm thrashing about," he said over the phone one day. He'd been e-mailing me vast tracts of notes from his trip to Antarctica—fifty thousand words worth, at one count. It was a fascinating mess. Plimpton, who once boxed with Archie Moore and tended goal for the Bruins, wasn't the type to let computers intimidate him, despite evidence that he was, to borrow from the title of his most famous book, out of his league. The process of electronic cutting and pasting flummoxed him, and files read like missing pages of the Dead Sea Scrolls. With the photo editor begging for something, anything that would allow her to start research, I flew down to New York to help George get organized.

We met in his commodious apartment above the *Paris Review*, which he edited for half a century, then walked in the rain to a nearby restaurant (not the Century Club, thank God) for lunch with Will. George ordered a Tom Collins.

Two hours later we had covered a lot of ground—very little of it, unfortunately, about Shackleton. We talked about September 11. George related how he had slept through the attacks because the night before, Paul McCartney had been over late, holding everyone rapt at the piano. Only George could make an "I slept through 9/11" story interesting.

After lunch George had to go give a talk or something, and I asked when we could sit down and work on the outline. "We're having a little pour tonight for an Indian journalist," he said. "Do come."

I arrived at nine o'clock to find the party winding down; a handful of *Paris Review* interns were lazily shooting pool in the game room. George was in his cluttered office, wearing a rep tie and blue blazer, watching a Celtics game. "Come on in," he said. "Pull up a chair," moving some piles of books around. "Get you a drink?"

We watched the game and talked about the Red Sox. (Though a native New Yorker, Plimpton retained a fondness for Boston teams from his Harvard years.) I inquired about a photo of Hemingway over his desk, and George told me about the time the great author socked him. "We were having lunch in Havana, and he was getting drunk," recalled George. "When he got drunk he got mean, and he kept insisting he wanted to box with me, right then. I said 'No I don't want to box now, we're eating lunch.' Finally he kicked out his chair, lunged across the table and popped me in the jaw. Extraordinary man."

I assured Will we were making progress.

The summer of 2002 went by and the book started taking shape. George went from "thrashing" to "plodding," which I took as a good sign. Still, fall came and started to merge into winter, and George seemed unable to deliver a finished manuscript. I offered to come down and help him for a week. "You can stay here" was his answer.

I booked a room in a nearby hotel, not wanting to impose on his family. The first morning I showed up, George was near tears. "I've lost a major section of the book," he said, gazing hopelessly at his computer. "It's gone. I'll never be able to reconstruct it."

George's computer screen looked like a Byzantine mosaic of Microsoft Word files. In fact the entire screen was nothing but file icons, layered in the hundreds like roof shingles. It was the bottom of the ninth, and Plimpton was out of pitches.

I sat down at his Macintosh and showed George how to use Command-F to search for text. As I suspected, the missing file was buried on his desktop. Then I showed him how to organize his files into folders, and how to store

them on his hard drive. For good measure I cleaned up his
e-mail lists, silently wishing my father (the same age as
George) would let me do the same for him. "Extraordinary," George said.

Every day we worked from 8:30 to 6, stopping only to
order roast beef sandwiches from a take-out menu. "Mine has
the *tomahto*," George would remind me when the food
showed up. And all day long, his intercom buzzed as his
assistant downstairs announced callers. "It's Conan O'Brien;
wants to know if you can come on the show tonight. Don't
forget you've got dinner at Nan Kempner's—black tie."
(George, the Manhattan penguin, glanced at his rumpled tux
on an arm of the sofa.) "It's Norman Mailer; he's in town." A
writer called for a book-jacket blurb; George composed it
over the phone. Another called inquiring about an overdue
check for something he'd contributed to the *Review*. "I'll get
it out to you today," promised George, who then summoned
the bookkeeper.

"This is embarrassing," George told her. "We must pay
this."

"Actually, George," she replied, "we owe other writers for
even longer."

"Yes, but he called me. Well, pay him out of my own
account."

Somehow we managed to finish *Ernest Shackleton* and have
some laughs in the process. The only time George got testy
was when I suggested a passage exploring Shackleton's motivations for leaving his wife behind all those years. "That's
surmising, and I don't do that," he said firmly. "I realize a lot

of writers make that their stock in trade, but I simply have never written that way." I was glad to see that George cared enough about this book to put his foot down.

Months later, George gone, I find the book holds up well—a respectable mix of conventional narrative and George's first-person adventures that, naturally enough, includes a frightening encounter with an angry sea lion. In short, it reads like a George Plimpton book. As an editor, I wish every author needed nothing more than to be strapped into a chair and shown Command-F. Extraordinary man.

49

It was a holiday weekend, and the Brattleboro Food Co-Op was mobbed. The harried New Yorkers who weekend in southern Vermont rarely leave their cares behind, and the aisles of organic wine, local apples and cage-free fertile eggs hummed with the tension of Important People Relaxing. I recognized the huffy frowns when my cart blocked an aisle, and the impatient tsk-ing from the woman behind me when I didn't have my money ready at the cashier. I felt like I was back in Manhattan.

Nobody was paying much attention to the bantamweight white-haired man in an apron wrapping cheese behind the counter. But he understood these people. Almost forty years earlier, he had directed a classic film about New York social manners called *Sunday in New York*, which starred Jane Fonda in her first screen role.

His name was Henry Tewksbury, but around Brattleboro he was known simply as the Cheeseman of Vermont—authority and author on the subject of fine cheese. Tewksbury died in 2003 at age eighty, and I suspect it will be some time before New England, not to mention Hollywood, sees another quite like him. As a fellow showbiz refugee in rural New England, I became drawn to Tewksbury and was privileged to know him in the last year of his life.

In the 1960s (using his real first name, Peter) Tewksbury directed five feature films—including not one but two Elvis movies (*Stay Away, Joe* and *The Trouble With Girls*). On television he won an Emmy for directing *Father Knows Best*, then directed the entire first season of *My Three Sons* before creating a short-lived cult series called *It's a Man's World*.

It's definitely a strange world, which may be the only way to explain how a Hollywood director found true happiness yelling "cut!" over a wheel of triple-cream Brie. Tewksbury's path from Beverly Hills to Brattleboro was not exactly linear, and involved the sort of drastic rethinking on the Meaning of Life that people did back in the '60s.

He grew up in Cleveland, the son of a manufacturer. After surviving Okinawa during World War II, Tewksbury mustered out in Seattle and decided to hang around. "I realized it was one of the few chances you get in life to start from scratch," he once told me. There he met and married his first wife; they relocated to Porterville, Cal., a sleepy Central Valley farm town, where Tewksbury talked his way into a job as a radio station manager despite having no experience: "I guess the guy was desperate," he told me one day. But in 1948 he founded a local community theater and spent the next seven years directing some hundred and fifty plays. By then the new medium of television was promising opportunity, and Tewksbury moved to Hollywood.

His first TV job was directing episodes of *Life With Father*, which earned him a reputation as a "family" director. "I did every father-and-kid show in Hollywood," he said.

But Hollywood's favorite family man had little time for his

own four children. "I was never home," he recalled. His shift into feature films added more responsibility. In *The Trouble With Girls*, Tewksbury managed to make one of the few decent Elvis movies. "I figured out that the way to get Elvis presentable was to surround him with good actors," he said. "So I picked New York actors, and boy he just rolled with them."

While Elvis was rolling, Tewksbury's marriage was crumbling. After meeting his second wife Cielle (now a Tai Chi instructor), he decided to raise a family the right way. "She pointed out that we probably weren't going to do it very well unless I got out of show business," he said. So in 1967 they moved to Vermont—chosen because it was one of the few states that was losing population. "It sounded like it was a progressive place," said Tewksbury. He bought a farm, and to wipe the slate truly clean, changed his first name. "Cielle and I are *now*-ists," he explained. "We have trouble living in the past."

Nonetheless, their back-to-the-land adventure lurched back and forth between Vermont and California, where the couple and their two children returned in 1977 to caretake a three-thousand-acre ranch near Cambria. There Tewksbury took up organic gardening, started a school, learned to milk a cow, and made his own "very bad" cheese. They returned to Vermont in 1990, buying a 1755 post-and-beam farm on 120 acres.

One day he offered to work at the Brattleboro Co-Op, starting as a dishwasher. (Income from television residuals freed him from the need for a high-stress job.) "When the woman running the cheese department left town, I volunteered," he said. "I started looking into people who made cheese locally, and there weren't many."

There are many more now. As manager of the cheese department for nine years, Tewksbury was on the front line of Vermont's artisanal cheese revolution—a rare farm-based agricultural success story of the 1990s. Tewksbury even wrote a book, *The Cheeses of Vermont* (Countryman Press), in which he combined profiles of artisanal cheesemakers with a travel guide to Vermont cheese farms and a primer on the process of fine cheesemaking.

That process is what fascinated Tewksbury. "I love the unpredictability of cheese," he told me once from behind the wheel of his Toyota pickup as we raced up Interstate Ninety-one. The Cheeseman spent a lot of time visiting cheese operations, and on that day we were off to the Westminster Dairy in nearby Putnam. Tewksbury was an exception to the rule that senior citizens drive slowly; despite a soaking rain, we passed other cars in a blur. "You don't know what you're gonna get with cheese," he went on, "and it takes a long time to find out. Sometimes it's wonderful, sometimes it's disastrous. Every time I open a new cheese, it's like a fresh miracle."

And a lot like life, in his case. His Emmy lies at the bottom of a Vermont swamp, where he tossed it years ago. "I've always had a lot of energy," he said. "Making movies was a wonderful way to use it, but so was washing dishes. Right now I'm doing what I like to do, which is cut cheese and talk to people. I'm a genuine cheesemonger is what I am."

50

C elebrities and Republicans complain that the media doesn't get it, but "it" is a moving target, as anyone who raises guinea hens knows. In fact, my four-month guinea hen nightmare can be blamed directly on a "media" report—more precisely, a passage in a book called *The Encyclopedia of Country Living* by Carla Emery (Sasquatch Books).

Being neither celebrated nor Republican, I won't tar and feather Ms. Emery (not that I'm short on feathers). In fact I am a longtime fan of her popular book. I hope it has made her wealthy; it has certainly made her a celebrity in some circles, and for all I know a Republican as well. The truth is, my sole complaint regarding this million-word tome centers on a single twenty-word sentence. Not wanting to sound churlish, allow me to first praise:

Emery's *Encyclopedia*, which began as a folksy newsletter in 1971 and evolved over almost a quarter century to the present manual, is a back-to-the-lander's bible, with practical advice on everything from heating with wood to burying your own dead, and homespun recipes from Pudding Popsicles to Mutton Burgers. The text is augmented by whimsical illustrations of the R. Crumb School: page 827 depicts the head of a pig with an X drawn through its forehead, below the helpful notation "Shoot here."

Emery herself doesn't fire many blanks. "Plain language empowers plain people," she writes. "If I wanted to write more obscurely, more formally and distantly, in the usage of the literati, I could. But I don't want to."

Nor does she want you to think she knows everything. Of goose livers, she writes, "make pâté de foie gras, for which I don't know the recipe, only that it's made out of goose livers." But Emery does claim to know a few things about guinea hens, and her writing on the subject is what persuaded me to raise these unusual birds.

Guinea hens are semi-domesticated flying fowl that are native to Africa (where they wander everywhere) and suited to a wide range of climates. Slightly smaller than chickens, their boxy profile gives them a hunchbacked look—a strangeness intensified by a hard, protruding crown on their head. The bird's spotted feathers, in shades of pearl, lavender, and gray, are prized by fly fishermen. The French, who call them *pintades*, prize their succulent dark flesh, which is about the closest you can get to the taste of wild game in a bird that you can raise.

That rich flavor comes from their diet, which consists mainly of bugs. No bland corn mash for these birds. They like all kinds of insects but are partial to Japanese beetles, and this is what intrigued me. My farm is infested with Japanese beetles. The grubs destroy my lawn every spring, and the beetles themselves go on to defoliate my roses and grapevines, before moving on to the peaches—and I mean the actual peaches, which they devour as soon as they ripen. So birds that eat beetles sounded like a great idea. The only downside to guinea hens appeared to be their loud, raucous call, which the legendary food writer Waverly Root once likened to a rusty windmill.

I did worry, however, that the guineas would find it hard to resist my grapes while feeding on the beetles. After all, songbirds devour them if I'm not diligent. But Emery wrote authoritatively in her *Encyclopedia:* "The guineas themselves are not fruit eaters and will not pick at fruit even if it falls on the ground." I was sold.

My guinea hens arrived on June 25, sixteen tiny chirping keets. Emery and several Web sites warned that guinea keets are extremely fragile, as we soon found out. Four died within a few days, and a fifth looked listless. My two boys decided to try and save it, and they spent hours coddling it under a heat lamp, and trying vainly to feed it with a dropper. After I made the observation that the little keet was no bigger than a golf ball, Whit promptly named it Golf Ball. When the tiny creature died, he cried.

The remaining eleven grew quickly in the shelter of the henhouse; within a few weeks they were leaping into the air to catch mosquitoes on the wing. The birds themselves couldn't fly yet, and their comical jumps entertained us. I felt certain our beetle troubles would soon be over.

After about two months the guineas started vocalizing—a sound for which no printed word can prepare you. It was so hellish, and so constant, that as a matter of public safety I could not recommend guinea hens to anyone who has neighbors within rifle range. Even with our windows closed, normal conversation became impossible. Sarah and

I had to shout at each other like American tourists in European restaurants.

Ominously, the guineas did not show much interest in the iridescent beetles that were now swarming on my grape leaves, preferring instead to peck around the ground underneath the vines. I tried flicking a few beetles into their path, but guineas don't let you get too close. Finally in late September, the grapes nearly ripe, I saw the guineas perched up in the vines, and I ran out to watch the slaughter. What I saw instead was a flock of guineas devouring my grapes.

The French, as many celebrities but few Republicans grasp, were right as usual. Guinea hens really do taste better than chicken. When I slaughtered them on November 1, Harper cheered. Whit said "The sound of death is very quiet," which he probably translated from Camus. All that remains is a tussock of spotted feathers in the woods, and a rock near my grapevines with the hand-lettered inscription: "R.I.P. Golf Ball."

51

The new Fox reality show called *The Simple Life* defies conventional TV criticism, in the way that black holes, by definition, defy visibility. The show's denominator is so uncommonly low, its premise so deliriously empty, that it ends up being funny in spite of itself—like a fart.

Except on *The Simple Life*, that pungent odor you're smelling comes from the cows. The idea, if it can be called that, is to relocate two ditzy blond party girls from Beverly Hills to a family farm in Altus, Arkansas. It's a given that when these exotic fish flop into the barnyard, wacky goings-on will ensue, critics will moan, and, thanks to recent real-life scandals involving both girls, viewers will tune in.

I did. As a former resident of Hollywood now down on the farm, I felt perversely obligated to slow down and take a look at this roadkill.

Enforced agrarianism is not a new concept in television (*Green Acres*) or real life (Pol Pot), but never have its victims inspired less sympathy than the Louis Vuitton–toting protagonists of *The Simple Life*. It goes without saying that Nicole Richie (the recently convicted, heroin-possessing daughter of singer Lionel), and Paris Hilton (the apparently malnourished hotel heiress/supermodel/amateur porn star whose very existence argues in favor of quintupling the estate tax) are, to put it charitably, empty vessels.

What's surprising (and distinguishes them from classic dumb blondes like Marilyn Monroe or Jayne Mansfield) is their utter lack of charm. "You know what? Fuck off!" is Nicole's wittiest riposte (the show's artful bleeping leaves no doubt what's being said), and both girls wear pants so low that their visible butt cracks are blurred out for prime-time audiences.

Their better-dressed hosts, the Ledings of Altus, seem like a pretty normal rural family. But compared to Paris and Nicole, they're like farmers in a Soviet mural. They bound out of bed at five, work hard and happily outdoors, eat hearty meals, and share a collective bathroom. There's no TV-watching pig named Arnold, and they're clearly not stupid.

But this is, after all, a Fox reality show, and the rarefied heights of dignity can be maintained for only so long. We return to earth in the barnyard, where things get earthy fast.

In the first episode, Paris and Nicole are asked by Grandma to help pluck chickens. They refuse and instead look on in horror. No surprise there; most Americans would recoil at the task, although preparing your own poultry for the table provides, in my experience, a deeply satisfying connection to the food cycle. More revealing is a later scene at the dinner table, where the girls push away their plates of homemade fried chicken in disgust.

Should the point be too subtle, the camera zooms in on a dinner plate, then cuts to a Hitchcockian montage of hanging birds, flying feathers, and falling cleavers. As the

Psycho-esque music swells, you half expect Grandma to burst into the dining room wielding a meat saw. What could be more disgusting, the show implies, than *eating an animal you just killed?*

Better, presumably, to eat battery-raised chickens pumped full of hormones, antibiotics, and substandard feed, then slaughtered and cut into "tenders" two thousand miles away and shipped on a truck for three days to a grocery store, where they sit wrapped in plastic for a week.

It turns out that fear of food is a running theme on *The Simple Life*. Episode two finds Paris and Nicole in the cow barn, where they have to fill milk bottles. "Is this milk, uh, pasteurized?" asks one (I can't remember which) as she eyes the bottles warily. Told it is not, she replies sagely: "I would never drink this," before spilling gallons of it all over the ground.

Of course she wouldn't drink it. She lives in California, where "health" authorities have harassed raw-milk dairy farms practically out of existence, even though the sanitary benefits of pasteurization have been wildly exaggerated. (As Sally Fallon points out in *Nourishing Traditions*, pasteurization destroys healthy natural organisms that actually protect milk from contamination. The process also kills basic enzymes that help humans digest milk; meanwhile, synthetic vitamin D2 added to pasteurized milk has been linked to heart disease.) Here in Maine, our family drinks nothing but unpasteurized milk from our neighbor's grass-fed cows, and my kids think grocery-store milk tastes disgusting.

But what's the point of whining over spilled milk? Lacking the genuine dangers of other reality shows, like poisonous beetles or treacherous waterfalls, the producers of *The Simple Life* (who almost certainly did not grow up on farms) fall back on the only remotely "gross" thing they can find: real food. In twenty-first-century America, eating the fresh, natural bounty of your own land is no longer one of life's basic pleasures. It's a TV dare.

Of course, TV is partly responsible for our culture's sad alienation from real food, thanks to the billions of dollars spent on advertising processed snacks and burgers. Rural folks watch TV as well, and from what I see at the local store, they eat as much junk as anybody else these days.

The fact is, television has made America as homogenous as grocery-store milk. Country dwellers like me who watched *The Simple Life* saw mostly the same commercials you did. One ad asked, "Is your hair pathetic and weak?" Another promised "five hundred bonus rollover minutes!" Out here in the boonies, we buy shampoo and cell phones too. As Richard Olney wrote in his classic book *Simple French Food*, "Simplicity—no doubt—is a complex thing."

Indeed, it's taken me five years to realize that you can have a pretty complicated life in the countryside, or live simply in Hollywood, if that's what you want. In the real world where no one is trying to sell you shampoo, the simple life is a state of mind, not the state of Arkansas.

At the end of episode two, our heroines make a break for it. It's midnight on Saturday, and they want some local action. Dressed in bustiers and micro-miniskirts, they sneak out of their bedroom and tear off in a pick-up truck, high beams blazing, as the credits roll. It's hard to imagine they'll find anything still moving at that hour in rural Arkansas, but stay tuned: this is TV, where everything is simple.

52

For anyone seeking a do-it-yourself life, away from the experts in New York and Hollywood who think they know better than you how to make money and have fun, I urge you to point your VW van (the one you painted yourself, with the underwear elastic for a carburetor spring and the two-by-four thingy that keeps the clutch from popping) straight in the direction of rural Maine.

The backcountry around me is Mecca for those who would do just about anything themselves rather than ask a pro. From local government to barn building, rural Mainers prefer their own version, no matter the result. It's the doing that counts, danger aside. For a state that recently turned down casinos, it's amazing how many rural Mainers with no masonry experience will gamble on constructing their own chimneys. The most commonly heard phrase out here is "How hard could it be?" (Followed later by the famous last line: "She's not goin' anywhere.")

It's a lifestyle I essentially endorse. Still and all, there are times when the experts are needed. I was thinking about this the other day as I stood, knife in hand, before two dead pigs, which were hanging from a tree and bleeding into the snow around my boots.

I was staring at the pigs, but what made me think of the

need for experts was a recent special town meeting called by our selectmen. It seems that our town spent more than was budgeted for legal costs last year—about ten thousand dollars more, quite a large sum in my town. Everybody knew why. A series of local land use decisions, most significantly the ongoing Lane case, meant lots of work for the town's attorney, whom we call the Eggman. Whenever an angry citizen stood up at a Lane hearing to gripe, the Eggman dipped into his suit jacket pocket and whipped out an egg timer. "You have three minutes!" he intoned, cranking the dial.

But this being rural Maine, not too many folks take kindly to experts bearing egg timers. Just about everybody keeps on talking until the hard-boiled stage, while the Eggman scowls and his ears turn red. Meetings in our town can get unruly, and the latest was a corker.

The meeting was required by law, which says that whenever selectmen spend beyond the approved town budget, they need to go back to voters and get permission. Statute aside, the vote is obviously pro forma; bills must be paid. Should voters elect not to pay the bill, the selectmen would simply take the money out of reserve funds, and there would be an asterisk on the town report.

But that was beside the point to the rubble rousers—including Bradley, whom the selectmen did not reappoint to the planning board when his term was up. By then, the Lane case had moved on—through our appeals board (which upheld the planning board's decision to grant the rock quarry but turned down the rock crusher) and up to state Superior Court. Of course, Lane isn't happy about losing its processing plants and rock crusher; it doesn't do them a lot of good to blast out car-sized pieces of granite if they can't crush them into stone and make a product. And we at the Land Association still maintain that the quarry itself is illegal under our zoning rules. The result is that both Lane and the Land Association are in court challenging different aspects of the town's decisions. It's an expensive mess that might have been avoided had Bradley handled things better from the beginning.

That's probably what the selectmen were thinking when they bounced him from the board. So for Bradley, it was personal. He showed up with his friends from the Rights Association at the town meeting, where they hoped they could make the selectmen squirm by voting down the payment to the lawyer. It was a classic small-town grudge match.

But we saw it coming, and we got out our own vote. In total about sixty people squeezed into our little community room, and the mood was as hard and cold as the metal folding chairs. The moderator asked for comments, and things got off to a bad start. "How do we know all these people live here?" asked a swarthy crew-cut guy in the back. "Are you checking them off on the voter rolls?"

Cheryl, our very able town clerk, tried to suppress a *gimme-a-break* glare and said "I know everyone in this room, Jim. We've never checked voter rolls for these meetings, and I don't believe it's a problem."

It went downhill from there, with lots of interruptions and accusations, until Janet got into it with Arlene. Arlene, who works down at Bradley's garage and also tends some of the cemeteries around town, is an outspoken member of the Rights Association. Janet is the outspoken wife of Dave, a member of the Land Association's executive board.

Arlene's family is one of the oldest in town, going back to the original, unruly band of settlers that squatted here in the colonial days and thumbed their noses at the English proprietors who owned the land; Janet is from the Bronx, where making rude noises is called cheering. It is neither a compliment nor an insult to suggest that from a pugilistic standpoint they are evenly matched.

After interrupting each other a few times, Arlene finally said "Janet, I'm sorry, I know you been sick, but if you wanna step outside and settle this right now, let's go!" And she jabbed a grease-stained thumb toward the door.

To say Janet had been sick was an understatement. A week earlier, doctors at Mass General had removed her cancerous kidney. So when Arlene challenged her to a fight, everyone gasped—except Janet, who jumped up and said "Let's go!"

"Sit down, Janet," said Dave, tugging her arm. To the relief of the selectmen, Janet sat down and the meeting went on. No blows were exchanged, and *yeas* outweighed *nays* by about a dozen votes.

Governor Baldacci believes we pay a steep price for those votes. He wants to consolidate local government, and in many ways he's right; the legal bills in my town—and a lot of anger—could be reduced if land use decisions were made by professional, regional planners, not volunteer townsfolk whose eyes glaze over at two hundred fifty-page mining applications and environmental impact studies.

The applicants show up with three hundred dollar an hour lawyers and hydro-geologists, against boards consisting of goat farmers and snowplow drivers. No wonder we get into trouble. No wonder we get socked with legal bills. It's not a fair fight.

But so long as we insist on do-it-yourself government (how hard could it be?), we will keep getting creamed by other people's experts. Baldacci is hopeful for change, but I'm not sure. As they say around here, she's not goin' anywhere.

53

I write this on my forty-seventh birthday, which is too far from forty to matter, and not quite close enough to fifty to care. It's a non-milestone that would merit no mention, were it not somehow so expressive of this dull, cold, dry winter. It's been so cold up here that some of my chickens got frostbite on their combs—a fairly common problem and the reason why cold-weather chicken breeds tend to be types with small combs, like my Barred Rocks and Rhode Island Reds. But they are not immune.

One frigid January morning I went out to the henhouse and found one of the Reds stiff from rigor mortis, or just frozen, on the floor under the roosting perch. She must have died in her sleep while roosting, then keeled over. I grabbed hold of her cold feet and carried her out to the woods. Chickens always seem heavier to me when they're dead; the weight and those scaly claws make them seem like the dinosaurs they descended from, and I had to swing my arm hard to heave her into the forest for the crows and coyotes.

It's a wonder the others are still laying eggs, but they do, every day. The eggs are big, too—what grocery stores would call jumbo—but they don't all make it into our kitchen. Some freeze and burst open before I can bring them in. Others break when I slip on the ice. When that happens, I let go of the eggs I'm carrying, so I can use my hands to catch my fall. I worry that someday, in the interest of saving an organic egg for a chocolate soufflé, I'll hold onto it and instead hit the ice hard on one of my forty-seven-year-old elbows. But so far I've managed to keep my priorities straight, despite my love of chocolate soufflés.

The ducks stopped laying eggs months ago, and without any water to swim in they occupy themselves by tearing feathers off the backs of the chickens. It's a nasty habit that leads to cannibalism, so now I have to figure out some way to isolate the chickens and ducks. But it's too cold for carpentry . . .

Ducks aren't the only ones with cabin fever. We went to Sunday River for a change of pace, but skiing exhausted me even more than usual. I felt like I had to will myself down the mountain, even though gravity was clearly on my side. On the chairlift, I looked around at all the people hurtling down the slopes on manmade snow and wondered why. I've been skiing on and off for most of my life, but suddenly it seemed like such an odd thing to do, stranger than tearing feathers off chickens' backs. When the chair crested the top of Aurora Peak, the wind rolling off Mount Washington slammed into me like a cannonball, and needles of sleet tattooed my face. My eight-year-old boy wailed. We skied down and went in for hot chocolate.

I began looking forward to a business trip south, even though I was only going as far south as New Jersey. *Reader's Digest* had hired me to write a story about the latest alleged killer nurse, a man who has admitted to dispatching some forty patients in hospitals around central New Jersey and eastern Pennsylvania. He claims, as many hospital killers do, that they were mercy killings, but of course the patients did not request any fatal injections. I drove around his old neighborhoods. He moved a lot, got divorced, had a girlfriend, but every place he lived since childhood looked the same—dense working-class enclaves of duplex houses sheathed in fake stone and aluminum siding. He was everything you could imagine, and less. "Quiet," said a neighbor. "Kept to himself," said another. "A coffee freak," said a co-worker. "It's always the quiet ones," said a cop. "What a surprise," said most people. What a surprise.

Back home, I went for a walk in my woods. I needed to be somewhere that wasn't the New Jersey Turnpike, but I was also trying to find my beaver. With the help of a state wildlife biologist, we finally got our beaver last spring. Although our pond was ideal beaver habitat, the beaver had other ideas, and he quickly disappeared. A few weeks later, while hunting for chanterelle mushrooms along a ridge overlooking a wetland, I stumbled on a stand of mature hardwoods that had been reduced to a pile of logs and sawdust. Twenty or more poplars as wide as a man's waist were chewed down to stumps, with fresh curls of woodchips scattered in piles. I figured the beaver had moved into the wetlands, and I wanted to find his lodge. That would have to wait until winter, however, when the wetland was frozen up and easy to traverse. So on my February birthday I headed out.

The thin layer of snow in the woods was hard and crusty, and my boots made so much noise as I crunched along that I couldn't hear the usual sounds of the forest in winter: the staccato drilling of the woodpecker, the chickadee's shrill cant, the porcupine rustling in the hemlock branches. I couldn't find the beaver lodge; my wetland is vast. "The government won't even let you fart in there," my grouchy father once intoned. "You might kill a mosquito."

I wondered why I felt the need to own all this land, which is roughly the size of the Vatican City. I wondered if the Pope ever felt that way. I paused on the surface of a frozen brook. A chickadee landed on a branch over my head, and I could hear the familiar humming of his wings. I heard water gurgling under the ice, perhaps a sign of spring. What a surprise.

54

The sap is indeed rising here, and with it the spirits of locals who glimpse some light at the end of winter's tunnel. Not that we're out of the woods yet—and those of us who tap maple trees are spending more time than ever there—but I detect around town a different philosophical take on life, so that even hardship is met with the levity of hope.

Down at the store, somebody was complaining how his septic line is still froze up, going on six weeks now. Hardly a laughing matter, but it didn't stop someone else from observing that his problem was simply that his shit wasn't warm enough, and maybe if his wife cooked more hot meals he wouldn't be in this mess.

This goes on all day, but some of us have work to do. For the first time since buying our farm five years ago, we got around to tapping our line of maple trees along the road. "The distilled essence of the tree" is how 19th-century naturalist John Burroughs described maple syrup. His words hint at something even more elemental than the wild, woody sweetness beckoning the backyard syrup enthusiast. At a time when practically every aspect of Western culture is defined by the mindless pursuit of excess (despite gathering evidence that we are out on a limb, so to speak), the process of reduction essential to syrup making is deliciously subversive. It takes about forty gallons of sap to make one gallon of syrup, so in that sense even the most ambitious sugarman is always thinking small. Make less, not more, says the sugarman. Make syrup, not war.

Of course we had practical motives for tapping our trees—namely the pressure of neighbors, who look suspiciously at those who "waste" sap by not tapping perfectly good trees. If the offender is a native, it's a clear sign of indolence; if he's from away—well, that just goes to show you. As our maple trees sit conspicuously along a main road, talk got started. One day last spring, Ron at the hardware store gave me the arched eyebrow and inquired: "You ever gonna tap them trees?" My throat stuck like a spoon in a syrup pan, and I stammered the usual excuses—no time, no equipment— before slithering home.

So this year I'm out there, drill in hand, hammer in belt, a pocketful of spiles and a wagonload of sixteen-quart galvanized pails. This year I'll show them—assuming I have the presence of mind to tap strictly maples. If you want to make a name for yourself in rural Maine, you could give the town a new library, or you could just hang buckets from a beech tree. A neighbor still talks annually about a previous resident of my house who tapped the big old oak in our front yard. That was in the 1950s. Tapping oak trees is a mistake not soon forgotten in these parts.

I knew which of my trees were maples, but I had a lot to learn about the work of sugaring. You need some equipment, for starters. You need pails, which cost about fifteen dollars each, new. I wanted some forty pails and wasn't about to spend six hundred dollars, so I found twenty used pails on the Internet for just four dollars each. Unfortunately they were in Wisconsin, and shipping added another fifty dollars— still cheaper than new. And the guy in Wisconsin had no used lids; you need lids to keep out bugs, bark, rain, snow and general crud. So he talked me into twenty new lids at three dollars each—and more shipping. Then came spiles—or spouts as they're called outside New England. The good kind are heavy cast aluminum and don't get all banged up from hammering. They cost a dollar eighty-five each at Husseys General Store.

I still needed about twenty more buckets and lids. Someone said Elmer was selling used buckets and lids. I drove down to Elmer's Barn, and found stacks of buckets at four dollars each. I kicked myself for paying fifty dollars in shipping to the guy in Wisconsin. But Elmer only had seventeen used lids (at a buck each). I bought all his lids, then pawed through the buckets to find seventeen good ones with no dents or rust. After spending a total of about three hundred fifty dollars, I was ready to set out thirty-seven buckets.

Then the sap starts flowing. How to boil it? When I finally put Earland Luce's sap pan to use, I realized I couldn't generate enough heat to keep all that sap boiling (it holds fifty gallons). It was useless. I dragged out my Bayou Classic outdoor cooker (fifty dollars), one of those propane burners that tailgate football freaks use to fry whole turkeys, and cranked it up. I put my biggest stockpot on top, filled it with sap, and let it rip.

It worked great, but my biggest stockpot holds only five gallons—enough sap to make about two cups of syrup. Out on the trees, my four-gallon buckets were filling faster and faster as the weather warmed and the sap ran stronger and stronger. The initial drip . . . drip . . . drip . . . in the buckets became *drip-drip-drip-drip-drip-drip-drip-drip*. It takes over two hours to boil down five gallons, and I was getting twice that much every day. It's not like you can go run errands while you're waiting: the sap could boil over and needs observation. Then came the propane bills—twelve dollars per fill-up, which was every day. As the expenses mounted, I began to wonder if sugaring was as truly reductive as promised; it was starting to seem about as minimal as a gold-plated Hummer.

You could always just drink the sap straight from the tree. It has a vaguely sweet flavor but mostly it tastes like sparkling clear spring water, naturally filtered. In *Stalking the Wild Asparagus*, Euell Gibbons (who made his own spiles from elderberry stems, curse him) recommends a tea made from maple sap and sassafras root—but then he also brushed his teeth with birch sap. One day while clearing low growth around my maple trees, I worked up enough thirst that the mere lack of a cup could not keep me from the cracking cold nectar in my buckets. I unhooked a bucket and raised it to my mouth like some giant racing trophy. But as I tipped it to my chapped lips, a disc of frozen sap the size of a barbell broke loose in the bucket and slammed into my nose. The sap exploded in a geyser across my face, and the bucket went *schlupp!* to the ground, filling my boots.

My consolation was that it meant less sap to boil. And my neighbors weren't watching. I hope.

I ended up selling Earland's sap pan for seventy-five dollars—twenty-five more than I paid for it three years earlier. At first I worried I was gouging the nice couple who bought it, but they offered my asking price without negotiating, so what was I supposed to do? Turning down their money would be something a guilty rich guy from away might do. But making a fifty-percent profit on an old piece of farm equipment was the mark of a true Mainer; I felt even better than Earland must have felt selling it to me for fifty. I was starting to get it.

55

Spring may soon be a reality up here—as opposed to *Spring: The Reality Show*, which we watch, not on TV, but splashed across the covers of magazines and catalogs. Could there really be places where lilacs are already in fragrant bloom, and outdoor luncheon tables sag under the weight of softball-sized peonies? Are people in The Rest of America seriously considering swimwear in April? Up here, even those of us who garden faithfully are still opening our doors in the morning and trying to plot a path along high ground to the car; the murky runoff that washes out our driveways and swirls in our cellars does not conjure days at the beach. We live on our own islands, although not the spruce-covered postcard versions that tourists envision when they think of Maine.

But we know spring is coming because the dump trucks are out again, growling like mean dogs as they grind through their gears up the Camden Road, their backs breaking under loads of fresh gravel for the parking lots of America. I wave at the drivers and they wave back, but it's a hollow greeting. I'm one of Those People, the people who support our town's mining ordinance. Many of the gravel guys belong to the Rights Association, which I think they should re-name Get Rid of Rules and Regulations, or GRRR, which is what their trucks sound like.

At least we still *have* the mining ordinance, which regulates run-of-the-mill mineral extraction and bans large strip mines altogether. We finally passed the ordinance in 2002, in reaction to the ongoing Lane case. So far, no one has interpreted the ordinance as being retroactive to Lane's application, which came in before the ordinance. But the Rights Association still tried to repeal it at the polls last month. They had many reasons why the two-year-old law was a bad idea, all of them easily refuted.

First they claimed the ordinance did not faithfully represent the town because it was voted in at town meeting (172 yes, 119 no), which is hard for some people to attend. (Town meeting can be thought of as a small New England community's legislature; it's where local laws are passed, except the legislators are the citizens themselves. And like the U.S. Congress, absentee votes are not allowed; the lawmakers must be present to debate and amend proposed laws.)

When it was pointed out that the town meeting vote represented seventy percent of the town's usual voters, they argued that the state already regulates mining through the Department of Environmental Protection, so why did we need our own ordinance? When the DEP replied that it actually encourages towns to write their own mining ordinances that reflect local concerns, they argued that the ordinance would prevent homeowners from tilling their gardens or removing rocks from their lawns. When it was observed that nothing in the ordinance prevented gardening and landscaping, they argued the ordinance would cost the town a lot of legal fees. When it was shown that the ordinance hasn't cost the town any legal fees, they growled and said just you wait, it will, it will.

It all sounded like a Bush press conference—and like Bush, the one argument they never made was the real one: they want to dig it all up and haul it away, and they don't want anybody else telling them how to do it. It made me angry that people could not be honest about their motivations, but I tried hard to spread the message that the ordinance gives our town more choice for the future, not less.

On election day I ran into a friend who sighed and said, "At this point, the town is going to get what it deserves." I swallowed hard at the thought, but she was right to trust in fate, which came down on our side. The repeal failed, by a landslide—156 yes, 321 no—preserving our ordinance and (presumably) putting further challenges to rest. And our newly drafted cellphone tower ordinance was voted in. Secure in the knowledge that our town was getting smarter, I went to work in my greenhouse and forgot about politics.

But then came Bush's press conference at the height of the Iraqi insurgence this spring. It was the first event I have watched on television since the Red Sox tanked in the last game of the American League playoffs last fall, and it was equally surreal. The President's hair looked uncharacteristically helmet-like ("It must have been a humid day in Washington," said Sarah) and the pattern on his silk tie produced a strange electronic moiré effect on my TV. The rippling psychedelic rainbow of colors flashing across his tie looked dangerous to pacemakers, and made it even less possible than usual to take him seriously.

Yet there he was with a straight face and a weird tie saying he would give his generals whatever they needed to win the war, while in reality farming out the conquest to tens of thousands of highly paid private mercenaries. In previous American wars, supplies were overseen by soldiers (remember Major Major in *Catch-22*?). In Iraq, we are paying private warehouse workers $100,000 annually. (Entry-level soldiers make about $13,000.)

Some of those private contractors are failed farmers—like Thomas Hamill of Macon, Mississippi, a dairy farmer on the skids who took a job driving a truck in Iraq for Kellogg, Brown & Root. He no longer has to worry about milk prices, but his family now has bigger worries; Hamill has been missing in Iraq for several days. (He was indeed captured by insurgents, but managed to escape. Go farmers!)

The day after the press conference, while starting eggplant seeds in my greenhouse, I wished one of the reporters had asked Bush what kind of country we have where a 43-year-old man can't make an honest living as a farmer and has to put himself in a war zone on the other side of the world to feed his family. My town may be getting smarter as the mud slowly recedes, but I worry more every day about my country.

Afterword

I'm standing in my kitchen on a Saturday in June, cutting up a duck. It's been cold; our woodstove is often still crackling until the Fourth of July. Sarah walks in. "Reagan just died," she says.

"Really?" Like many people, I had more or less forgotten he was still alive.

"Funny," she goes on, "when he was President I thought he was scary and evil. But compared to Bush, he seems so nice."

Perceptions do change, including the perception I once harbored that June was summer. But after five years in the Maine woods, I'd have to say my biggest change has been the way I perceive of a life well lived.

When we moved here, I thought I knew what I wanted, and how things would probably go. Adversity like the strip-mine fight (still in the courts after three years) could not have been predicted, nor could I have envisioned my run for public office. But accepting that things don't always turn out how you expect is, in a sense, beside the point; more important was a change inside myself (also unforeseen) that allowed me to see the process as mattering more than the goal itself.

Like most American guys, I grew up learning to set goals and achieve them: win the game, get the job, marry the girl. It's now possible for me to see my back-to-the-land adventure as another in a long series of personal goals. Could it be that my rejection of the modern go-go lifestyle was merely a decision to go-go in a different direction? Buy the farm, plant the crop, build the barn. "How do you get so much done around here?" asked my father-in-law one day. Go-go-go.

Clearly, a genuine change would not constitute trading in the Miata for a John Deere, but rather casting loose my goal-oriented mindset. That, it turns out, has been even harder than growing watermelons in Maine.

But events have conspired to hasten my education. The simple rhythms of rural life, unfolding beneath a cosmic blanket of stars, offer a constant reminder that I am not in charge. I help my kids display our roadside crops with pride, and I no longer care if buyers don't know who I "really" am. This is who I really am.

Running for selectman reinforced my sense of place, and also forced me to listen. I may not agree with some of my fellow townsfolk, especially on issues of land use, but for the most part I can appreciate their concerns. I even like Bradley.

I know that if the members of the Rights Association still farmed, like their ancestors, they would be better stewards of their land; they would realize that their "rights" are both infinite and non-existent—based not on land-use regulations passed by "people from away" but on the laws of nature that govern us all, and that require us to respect that with which we have been temporarily entrusted. Talk to them as individuals for any length of time and you learn how much they still know about working the land—how they instinctively know what's bad for the soil and the water, and what works best. For even though few of them farm (it's mostly us newcomers who do that, and then mostly as a sideline), my town's natives are only a generation removed from men and women who quite literally lived by what they could raise. They have much to share, if only our goals didn't get in the way.

Our town's isolation breeds mistrust of those from away, but it also encourages surrender to higher powers. Daily schedules must constantly adapt to our distance from stores, or friends, or schools. The twenty-two mile drive to the Ashwood Waldorf School is one reason Sarah no longer teaches there, and our children no longer attend. Instead, this fall we begin our second year of homeschooling. That adventure is another subject, for another day, but there too Sarah and I have both come to realize there is no "goal"—only a constant process of learning.

We still have our goals, of course, material and otherwise: the timber-framed barn, the sheep operation, the trails in the woods, happy kids, no strip mine, a new John Deere tractor. But increasingly we wake up every day and wave the white flag. Will I ever find a guy who can dig a pond? Do our kids actually learn anything at home? Is there a better farm, closer to town? How many years can my knees hold up? Will Felicia eat Swiss chard? What, after all, is the point of this whole adventure?

Thomas Jefferson once wrote: "Cultivators of the earth are the most valuable citizens." After five years with my hands in the soil, I know what he means. People with a stake in the future of their land care deeply about their communities. (I certainly never considered running for office when I lived in New York, or Hollywood.) And communities are where democracy begins. Jefferson knew that a rootless society, one in which work loses its meaning, was dangerous. Living and working on my own land has made me a better citizen.

Where does that leave the rest of the country? Does everyone load up the Volvo and move to Vermont, or Montana, or the Upper Peninsula? Of course not. But a good long break might be in order—perhaps one of those monthlong vacations they get in Europe, where capitalism is less goal-oriented.

I actually feel that if I moved back to the big city tomorrow, I would be a better citizen there too. I certainly wouldn't yell at waiters. But it took getting away to get it. It took living by my own wits, under the same roof with wife and children day and night, to realize that I am more than a replaceable part in someone else's machine, even if I sometimes feel like a draft animal. At night I fall into bed exhausted from my labors, but never frustrated by my inconsequence. I furl the white flag for eight hours, and dream contentedly of tomorrow's battle.

So there's a process: To both fight and surrender in the same moment. It's as good a recipe as any for living well in the twenty-first century, and I'm beginning to see how you can make it anywhere.

Acknowledgements

P eter Kadzis—editorial director of the *Boston Phoenix* media empire and a friend for the last quarter century (may God help us)—gets credit for giving me permission to do this at all. Sam Smith and Sam Pfeifle of the *Portland Phoenix* encouraged and indulged. Chad Verrill inspired me with his original artwork for the columns in the newspaper.

Will Balliett at Carroll & Graf was the first person to get it, and I'm so lucky to know him. What a guy. For that I thank Clint Willis, who also encouraged me to leave New York and to have no fear. Nate Knaebel at Carroll & Graf suggested many improvements, as did my agent, Stacey Glick.

Could there be an intelligent back-to-the-land movement without the writings of Wendell Berry? Not in my book. Readers could do no better than his seminal 1977 work, *The Unsettling of America*, reprinted in 1996.

I kneel at the altar of my town. I bow to friends, opponents, incumbents, and neighbors, for their honesty, good humor, and grace. What a great place to live.

Whit, Harper and Sarah: Without you I'm something—but not the guy who wrote this book.

About the Author

Max Alexander used to be a successful magazine and newspaper editor in New York and Hollywood. He now lives with his wife and two children in Maine, where he is a failed politician and a borderline farmer.